NEEDLEWORK
from **PATTERNS**
The Metropolitan Museum of Art

NEEDLEWORK
PATTERNS
from
The Metropolitan Museum of Art

SUSAN SIEGLER

New York Graphic Society *Boston*

TO BILL

Diagrams by Susan Siegler

Photographs by William F. Pons,

Walter Yee, and Allan Rodney

Designed by Margaret Dodd

Library of Congress Cataloging in Publication Data

Siegler, Susan.
  Needlework patterns from the Metropolitan Museum of Art.

  Bibliography: p.
  1. Needlework—Patterns. 2. Canvas
embroidery—Patterns. I. New York (City). Metropolitan
Museum of Art. II. Title.
TT753.S495 1976   746.4′4   76-10097
ISBN 0-8212-0639-7

First edition

New York Graphic Society books are published by
Little, Brown and Company. Published simultaneously in
Canada by Little, Brown and Company (Canada) Limited
Printed in the United States of America

Contents

List of Patterns 6

Acknowledgments 8

Preface 9

INTRODUCTION 11

Embroidery on Canvas 12

About canvas; needles; yarns; frames; preparing the canvas;
working a design from a charted graph.

Embroidery on Other Types of Fabric 15

About fabrics; needles; yarns; frames; enlarging an embroidery
pattern; transferring a design to fabric; working from a stitch and
color chart.

A Few Comments about Stitchery 18

Threading the needle; starting and ending off; ripping out; how
to achieve even, smooth stitches.

THE PATTERNS 21

A GALLERY OF STITCHES 143

*Selections for Further Reading
and Reference* 184

The Patterns

AUTUMN LEAVES, *from a needlepoint chair seat, American, eighteenth century.*

Pattern 22   *Color illustration* 25

RAINBOW GEOMETRIC, *from a needlepoint sampler, probably Italian, dated 1760.*

Pattern 33   *Color illustration* 27

STILL LIFE WITH GRAPES, *from a tapestry-woven decorative square, Egyptian (Coptic), probably fifth–sixth century A.D.*

Pattern 36   *Color illustration* 26

FANTASTIC FLOWERS, *from a crewel-embroidered hanging, French, eighteenth century.*

Pattern 42   *Color illustration* 28

PASTORAL LANDSCAPE, *from a needlepoint picture, American, about 1750.*

Pattern 46   *Color illustration* 29

GRAPEVINES IN INTERLACING BANDS, *from a tapestry-woven ornament, Egyptian (Coptic), probably fourth century A.D.*

Pattern 52   *Color illustration* 30

PAIR OF PEACOCKS, *from a crewel-embroidered bed hanging, English, late seventeenth century.*

Pattern 56   *Color illustration* 31

SACRED LOTUS, *from an embroidered rank badge, Chinese, nineteenth century.*

Pattern 60   *Color illustration* 32

ALONG THE RIVER BANK, *from an embroidered silk panel, Chinese, late Ming dynasty, seventeenth century.*

Pattern 64   *Color illustration* 74

FLOWERING THISTLE, *from an embroidered sampler, English, first half of the seventeenth century.*

Pattern 70   *Color illustration* 73

INDIANS IN FEATHERED HEADDRESSES, *from a loop-stitch embroidery, Peruvian, Late Chimu Culture, A.D. 1100–1400.*

Pattern 81   *Color illustration* 75

CRICKET ON A CHINESE CABBAGE, *from an embroidered needle case, Chinese, nineteenth century.*

Pattern 84   *Color illustration* 76

CHINESE MOSAIC, *from an embroidered fan case, Chinese, eighteenth–nineteenth century.*

Pattern 88   *Color illustration* 77

PUPPIES, *from a tambour-embroidered carpet, American, dated 1835.*

Pattern 92 *Color illustration* 78

KITTENS, *from a tambour-embroidered carpet, American, dated 1835.*

Pattern 94 *Color illustration* 79

EARTH-COLORED PEASANT REPEAT, *from a peasant costume, Albanian or Montenegrin, eighteenth–nineteenth century.*

Pattern 99 *Color illustration* 80

FLOWER GARDEN WITH WILD STRAWBERRIES, *from a petit point purse, American, about 1760.*

Pattern 102 *Color illustration* 115

ROSES AND CARNATIONS, *from an embroidered altar frontal, Italian, seventeenth–eighteenth century.*

Pattern 106 *Color illustration* 116

PARROT IN A PEAR-SHAPED TREE, *from a pear-shaped purse, English, first quarter of the eighteenth century.*

Pattern 110 *Color illustration* 113

PEASANT HAPPINESS DESIGN, *from a peasant blouse, Albanian or Montenegrin, eighteenth–nineteenth century.*

Pattern 121 *Color illustration* 114

PERUVIAN PUMA GOD, *from a tapestry-woven costume, Peruvian, Tiahuanaco II Culture, about A.D. 700–800.*

Pattern 124 *Color illustration* 117

FLOWERS OF THE FOUR SEASONS — 1, *from an embroidered sleeveband, Chinese, nineteenth century.*

Pattern 130 *Color illustration* 118

FLOWERS OF THE FOUR SEASONS — 2, *from an embroidered sleeveband, Chinese, nineteenth century.*

Pattern 132 *Color illustration* 119

TURKISH PEACOCK, *from an embroidered bedspread, Albanian (Janina), eighteenth century.*

Pattern 138 *Color illustration* 120

Acknowledgments

Special thanks are due many members of the Metropolitan Museum of Art's staff, who gave generously of their time and interest. I am particularly grateful to Bradford Kelleher, the Museum's Publisher, for his encouragement and support of this book from its conception to completion; to my associates in the Production Department for their enthusiasm and helpful suggestions; to Jean Mailey, Curator in Charge of Textiles, who shared her expertise by contributing invaluable comments and ideas; to Barbara Teague, Assistant in the Department of Textiles, for helping me in many ways; to Bill Pons, Walter Yee, and Allan Rodney for their excellent photographs, which enhance our appreciation of both the original textiles and the adaptations; to Shari Lewis for her assistance in researching the English embroideries; and to Morrison Heckscher for providing the beautiful eighteenth-century Queen Anne-style chair from the Museum's American Wing as a mounting for the adaptation *Autumn Leaves*.

My sincerest thanks to Al Mintz of Mazaltov's Inc. for his advice and information; to Bernice Barsky for reading and commenting on my stitch instructions; to Rita Klein for her suggestions on design preparation; and to the following talented needleworkers who worked the sample embroideries: Irene Phillips, Marge Bier, Hilda Attarian, Bernice Barsky, Susan Brown, Melanie O. Greco, and Gail Young.

I am grateful to my editor, Betty Childs, for her inspiring suggestions, and to Margaret Dodd, one of the most talented and patient designers I've ever worked with. Love and special thanks to my husband Bill for his understanding and for providing me with that extra encouragement at just those right moments.

Preface

Over the years The Metropolitan Museum of Art has received many requests for needlework patterns based on designs in its collections. Borrowing and adapting designs from the work of others is certainly not a new concept; needleworkers, artists, and craftsmen in all media have done this throughout history. It is a creative way of keeping design traditions alive and fresh, for a design removed from its original context may often be appreciated in a totally new way.

All of the patterns presented in this book were inspired by tapestries and embroideries in the Museum's collections. The adaptations are not necessarily of the rarest or the most famous pieces, for the models were chosen primarily to delight, teach, and challenge today's needleworker. In making the selection, I tried to gather a group that would convey a sense of the great range of designs produced by needleworkers throughout the centuries. These are not provided simply as exercises in imitation, but as a way of transmitting a variety of embroidery techniques and attitudes toward design and the use of color. In all cases I tried to retain the character of the Museum's textiles in the process of adapting them for presentation in a book. This meant that many otherwise wonderful embroidery designs had to be rejected since they required oversimplification to make them readable and workable. By choosing examples from different cultures and civilizations, I tried to show that each design has a unique story to tell. Some were clearly dictated by myth or tradition and reflect the beliefs of a particular society; others mirror the fashions of their day; still others are personal creative statements made by anonymous hands.

The patterns are arranged without regard for chronological sequence. This was done intentionally to heighten the impact of each design, and to avoid having it viewed solely as a historical document. I hope that through this presentation these inspirations from the past may find new meaning today.

S. S.

Introduction

These needlework patterns are for embroidery on canvas (needlepoint) or on other types of fabric. The term "embroidery" is generally used to describe the process of applying decorative stitches onto fabric. Developing and working an embroidery design can be an exciting and rewarding project, but to create a beautiful piece takes some knowledge, a little patience, and lots of enthusiasm. Before beginning any one of these projects, you might review the ways of handling the materials to achieve the best finished results, and the various methods for preparing and working an embroidery design.

Embroidery on canvas

ABOUT CANVAS

Most embroidery canvas sold today is made of cotton that has been treated with starch to give it body. It is available in several weights, ranging from a very fine canvas, with 27 mesh to the inch, to a coarse 3-mesh canvas. The most popular mesh sizes for needlepoint are #10, #12, #13, and #14. The smaller 20-mesh canvases are used for delicate petit point and the larger #4 and #5 for rugs and wall hangings. Canvas can be purchased in a variety of colors; white and tan (unbleached) are the most commonly used. The names applied to the canvas types — mono and penelope — refer specifically to the way in which the canvas threads are woven. I used both types for my needlepoint adaptations.

Mono canvas is woven with single vertical and horizontal threads. A mesh on mono canvas is the point of intersection of a vertical and a horizontal thread. The mesh size refers to the number of mesh in one inch; the greater the number of mesh, the finer the canvas. I used #10 mesh and #13 mesh for my adaptations on mono canvas.

Penelope canvas is woven with double vertical and double horizontal threads. The two warp (vertical) threads are woven very close together; the two woof threads are spaced slightly apart. A mesh on penelope canvas is the point of intersection of double vertical and double horizontal threads. The mesh size for penelope also indicates the number of mesh to the inch. My adaptations worked on penelope were done on 11-mesh canvas.

Both types of canvas should be worked with the selvage on either the right or left side. This gives better mesh coverage and helps to reduce the amount of distortion caused in working the canvas, since the stitches are then worked "with" the canvas grain, not against it.

ABOUT NEEDLES

The needle used for canvas embroidery is called a tapestry needle. Unlike the usual sewing needle, it has a large, elongated eye and a blunted point. The needle size you select will depend on the weight of the canvas being used:

> For 10-mesh canvas, use a #16 tapestry needle
> For 12-mesh canvas, use a #18 tapestry needle
> For 13-mesh canvas, use a #20 tapestry needle
> For 18-mesh canvas, use a #22 tapestry needle

As with canvas weights, the higher the number of the tapestry needle, the finer it is.

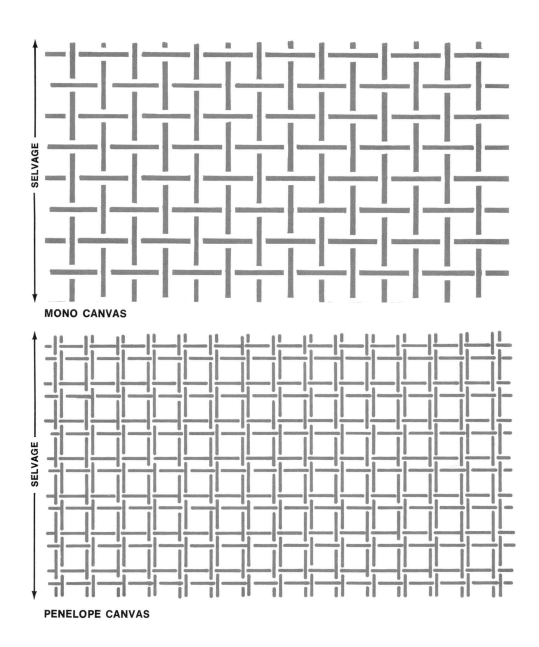

MONO CANVAS

PENELOPE CANVAS

ABOUT YARNS

Many types of yarn are suitable for canvas embroidery. These include crewel yarn, tapestry yarn, cotton and silk thread. Since I worked only in crewel-type yarn and cottons, I will describe these in some detail.

WOOLS Wool has been used in embroidery for at least a thousand years. The word "crewel" has its roots in sixteenth-century England, where it was first used to describe any worsted yarn made of two threads. Actually, all embroidery worked with two-ply wool may be referred to as crewelwork, although today we normally associate the term with a style of embroidery reminiscent of the exotic floral patterns of seventeenth- and eighteenth-century England. The type of wool I used throughout is Persian wool, which is a two-ply yarn made of three loosely

13

twisted strands. Paternayan's brand is the most lustrous, wears the best, and is available in an extraordinary range of colors. It may be purchased prepackaged in small 8½-yard skeins or in larger 40-yard skeins. Many stores will sell Paternayan wool by individual three-twist strands, each strand cut to working lengths of one yard. Use Persian wool full strength (all three strands) on 10-mesh mono canvas. The strands separate very easily for use on finer mesh canvas. If only two strands are required, as for 13- or 14-mesh mono canvas, then gently pull away one strand and use the remaining two. There is no waste, since you can match up the single leftover strand with a single leftover strand from the next group.

COTTONS The loveliest embroidery cottons are those manufactured by the French company D.M.C. (Dollfus-Mieg & Cie). Where I wanted to approximate the texture and sheen of silk threads, I used D.M.C. six-strand mercerized cotton. This type of cotton is available in the greatest variety of colors and may be purchased at most embroidery shops and at embroidery counters of major department stores. It comes prepackaged in 8.7-yard skeins. Since the cotton has a tendency to twist as it is worked, it should be cut into short, manageable working lengths of about 12 to 14 inches.

ABOUT FRAMES

The use of a frame for canvas work is really a matter of individual preference. The canvas can be stapled to artists' stretchers or it can be used in a hoop or square frame. Keeping the canvas taut while it is being worked helps prevent distortion and unnecessary handling. However, if you are more comfortable working without a frame, do so, for blocking will restore the shape of the canvas after the embroidery is complete.

PREPARING THE CANVAS

Since canvas is sold from rolls of varying widths, it has to be cut to size for each project. Try to leave one selvage intact (or mark that side before cutting) so that you can tell the proper direction for working the canvas (remember, the selvage should be on either the right or left side). After the canvas has been cut, take one-inch masking tape and fold it over the raw edges to prevent them from raveling and to keep the wools from snagging.

WORKING A DESIGN FROM A CHARTED GRAPH

The charted graph eliminates the necessity of hand-painting a design on canvas — which can be very time-consuming and costly — and allows you to embroider directly on a blank canvas. The graph is an embroidery recipe with stitch-by-stitch

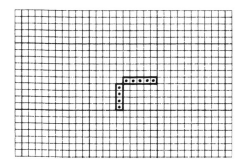

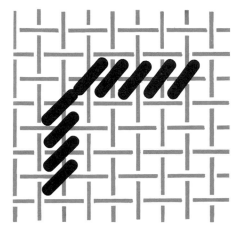

directions. For a symmetrical or geometric pattern, like the Coptic design on page 30 or *Chinese Mosaic* (page 77), it isn't possible to alter the directions without spoiling the "dish" — so count these carefully. With a more free-flowing design, like *Flower Garden with Wild Strawberries* (page 115), if you miss a stitch, or are off a few stitches here and there, it really won't make too much difference to the total effect. The charts for canvas embroidery are drawn on graph paper; every tenth line is heavier, making counting much easier. Some embroiderers like to pencil corresponding ten-marks directly onto the canvas, and others use safety pins or basting thread for guides. I just count, since my eyes quickly adjust to the scale. If you do decide to mark the canvas, do it lightly, and use a 4H pencil, which doesn't smear and erases easily if an error is made.

When working from a charted graph it is important to remember that each box on the graph represents one *mesh* on the canvas and not a space, or hole, on the canvas. Therefore when counting nine boxes on the graph, you must count nine mesh on the canvas. As for the colors, the various hues are designated on the chart by different tones or symbols. If you find this confusing at first, tape a small piece of yarn next to its appropriate symbol as a visual reminder. Another handy way of working is to have the chart photostated (you can have it enlarged at the same time if you prefer to work from larger grids) and lightly color in the various sections with colored pencils. Be sure that the colors don't obliterate the grid lines.

To estimate the finished size of an embroidery worked from a charted graph, divide the total number of boxes along each side by the number of mesh to the inch in the canvas being used. For example, if the design measures 200 x 200 mesh, the finished embroidery will be approximately 20 x 20 inches if worked on 10-mesh canvas and approximately 15¼ x 15¼ inches if worked on 13-mesh canvas. Finished sizes can only be approximated because of the thread variations in the canvas.

Embroidery on other types of fabric

ABOUT FABRICS

Almost any fabric with a plain or a basket weave, like cotton, linen, wool, burlap, silk, velvet, and some synthetics, can be embroidered. The selection of fabric will depend on the way the finished embroidery will be used and the type of stitches that are planned. For example, an embroidered chair seat should be worked on a foundation fabric that will wear well, but an embroidered picture can be done on a lighter-weight fabric. Certain stitches, such as Cross stitch or Darning stitch, can be done only on even-weaves. All my adaptations not worked on canvas are on linen — either twill or basket weave.

ABOUT NEEDLES

There are two types of embroidery needles generally used for fabrics other than canvas: crewel needles and chenille needles. Crewel needles have short eyes and pointed tips and are available in sizes ranging from a very fine #10 to a large #1. Chenille needles are shorter and have large, elongated eyes and pointed tips. These are sized from the tiny #26 needle to a large #13. When selecting a needle, choose a size that will penetrate the fabric easily and one that leaves a large enough hole in the material to allow the yarn to pass easily. For the adaptations worked on linen twill, a tapestry needle was used to obtain a slightly larger hole in the fabric.

ABOUT YARNS

The yarns suitable for canvas embroidery can be used on other fabrics as well. My samples on linen were worked either in Persian wools or D.M.C. cottons. When using wools, I separated the three strands and worked with a single strand. For the samples stitched in cottons, two types of D.M.C. threads were used. The first is the six-strand mercerized cotton that has already been described. The strands were usually separated into groups of three or four strands to achieve a finer thread. The easiest way to separate six-strand cotton is to cut it into working lengths first, then separate the strands from the center out toward the ends; if you try to pull it apart from top to bottom, it will knot and twist. The second type of cotton used is the D.M.C. pearl, which is a twisted yarn that cannot be separated. It is available in several weights; I used #5, which comes prepackaged in 27.3-yard skeins.

ABOUT FRAMES

Most embroiderers find it essential to use a frame for fabrics other than canvas — I agree. Embroidery frames are available in all shapes and sizes. If you have a favorite kind, use that. I find the easiest method of keeping the fabric taut for stitching is to mount the material onto artists' strips or stretchers. It takes a few extra minutes to prepare, but it saves the effort of having to remove the frame each time the work is set aside. Since the material is handled so little, it remains fresh and unwrinkled, which is helpful later on in finishing. Stretchers can be a great money-saver, too, for if the finished embroidery is to be framed, no additional mounting is necessary if you selected strips of the proper size. To mount fabric on stretchers, first assemble the wooden strips. Be sure that the corners are perfect right angles. Using an office stapler opened flat, begin by stapling the fabric to the center of the top strip; place about three staples along the edge of the top stretcher near the center, then pull the fabric taut and put three corresponding staples along the bottom edge. Then place three staples along the right side near the center, pull the fabric taut and do the same along the left side. Now go back to the top, put in a few more staples working from the center out, and staple the bottom and the sides in the same way. Work all sides until the fabric is completely taut. Staples will not harm most fabrics, but I would not recommend this method for delicate silks.

ENLARGING AN EMBROIDERY PATTERN

Since many of the pattern drawings are reduced to fit the book page, they require enlargement before transferring onto fabric. The easiest, and certainly the quickest, way to enlarge the design is to have it done mechanically by a photostat service. I find other methods very tedious for designs with any amount of detail — save your efforts for the embroidery! The dimensions for enlargement are indicated for each pattern. Of course you can provide your own dimensions if you plan to work the pattern in a size that differs from that of the sample. When ordering a photostat, request "matte finish, enlarged to size." You can ask for either a positive or negative image, since they work equally well — inquire which is less expensive in the desired size.

TRANSFERRING A DESIGN TO FABRIC

Once the design is enlarged, trace the outline on a piece of medium-weight tracing paper with a light-colored felt-tip pen. Place the foundation fabric, right side up, on top of a large blotter, heavy paper, or a thin piece of cardboard. Put the tracing over the fabric with the outline on top. Be sure to center it carefully. Now slip a piece of dressmaker's carbon between the tracing and the fabric; the shiny side of the carbon should face the fabric. Use the blue carbon for light-colored fabrics and white for darker shades. Secure this neat sandwich by putting a few staples along the top about ½ inch down from the edge and a few more along the sides near the top. The lower half of the sandwich remains open so that the layers can be lifted occasionally to check to see how well the outline is transferring. To keep the blotter from shifting, tape all four corners to a hard working surface. Now begin to retrace the design; use a medium-tip ball point pen to get the best line. Since the ink is a contrasting color to the felt-tip line, it is easy to tell which areas have been retraced. After a small area has been completed, lift the layers to see if the proper pen pressure is being applied; then continue tracing until the entire pattern has been transferred.

Animal woodcuts from a pattern book by Giovanni Andrea Vavassore, Venice, circa, 1530. Harris Brisbane Dick Fund, 1932.

WORKING FROM A STITCH AND COLOR CHART

The stitch symbols and letters indicate the type and placement of the stitches. The symbols are drawn in the correct working direction for the stitches. In some cases arrows are provided to show stitch direction. The symbols *do not* indicate the number of stitches to be worked; do as many stitches as necessary to fill an area. The numbers provided represent individual colors and indicate color placement.

A few comments about stitchery

THREADING THE NEEDLE

It is not always possible to thread a needle in the ordinary way with yarn of several thicknesses. To accomplish this easily, take the strand in hand and fold about an inch of one end over the thickest part of the needle. Pinch the strand tightly around the needle using your thumb and index finger, then pull the needle free. Still holding the pinched yarn, push the eye of the needle toward it to pass the yarn through. If the yarn separates and doesn't penetrate the needle properly, either it hasn't been pinched tight enough or it is too thick for that particular needle.

STARTING AND ENDING OFF

When starting a thread on canvas, reserve about an inch below the fabric and anchor it in on the underside with the first few stitches. Or bring the needle up about two inches ahead of the starting point and make a few basting stitches back to the starting stitch; the beginning stitches are covered over as the work progresses. When using fabric other than canvas, make a small knot at the end of the strand and begin with the knot on the *face* of the embroidery by going in with the needle a few inches from the starting point. When the strand is complete, clip the knot, rethread the loose end and run it through some stitches on the wrong side. Knots on the back of the work are not recommended since they create lumps on the surface of the embroidery — this is not only unattractive but an uneven surface will always wear poorly. However, if the finished embroidery is to be hung, fine knots on the back will do no harm. Regardless of the foundation fabric used, always try to begin and end the yarn by running it through same colored stitches on the wrong side, and clip all loose ends as you go along to avoid tangles as new stitches are worked.

RIPPING OUT

An embroidery done by an experienced needleworker usually appears faultless, but the fact that errors aren't noticeable doesn't mean that there weren't any — it indicates that they weren't *ignored*. Everybody has to do some ripping out; just remember to *unthread* the needle before removing unwanted stitches, and wherever possible, use the eye rather than the point of the needle to loosen them.

HOW TO ACHIEVE EVEN, SMOOTH STITCHES

When working on canvas, try to establish a rhythm to the stitching. Use a relaxed hand and don't yank the yarn after the needle is passed through the canvas. The stitches should always be bouncy, never tight. When working on linen or other fabrics, use the weave of the material as a guide to help achieve even stitches. During embroidery, all yarns have a tendency to twist; it is important to correct the twist to achieve smooth stitches. Rotate the needle in the opposite direction to untwist, or let the needle hang free and the yarn will usually untwist itself.

Note: If the materials and accessories needed to work the patterns provided are not available locally, further information may be obtained by writing to Mazaltov's Inc., Department B, 61 West 23rd Street, New York, New York 10010.

Woodcuts on pages 2, 10, 20, 142 from 1908 facsimile of 1530
Paris edition of pattern book by Francesco Pellegrino. Transferred from the library, 1922.

Woodcuts on pages 15 and 18 from a pattern book by Peter Quentell, Cologne, 1544. Rogers Fund, 1922.

Ornamental woodcuts on pages 5, 8, 9 from a pattern book by Hermann Gülfferich, Frankfurt, 1553. Harris Brisbane Dick Fund, 1923.

Woodcuts on pages 12 and 13 from a pattern book by Matio Pagano, Venice, 1556. Harris Brisbane Dick Fund, 1929.

The Patterns

I use "adaptation" to describe these patterns, since in many cases I've changed the scale of the Museum's original or simplified a design that was originally worked on extremely fine mesh. In all cases, however, I've tried to maintain or capture the character of the Museum's piece. Some time ago I designed a needlework kit for the Museum that was a needlepoint adaptation in wools of a Chinese silk embroidery. One woman commented to me that if she had realized from the first that the original was worked in silk she would have used silk threads as well, but unfortunately she began working with wools before she had read the historical data accompanying the kit. With that story in mind, I'd like to emphasize here that the dimensions, materials, and stitch techniques for each Museum object are provided in the caption for the illustration of the original.

The colors listed with each pattern are the result of hours spent matching and checking sample colors against the original textiles; in cases where I was matching wool colors to silks, they are naturally approximations. Wherever possible, the adaptations are worked in the same stitches as the original embroideries. In some cases I chose designs originally in simple tapestry weaves, since they adapt so well to needlepoint stitches.

Autumn Leaves

Canvas-work chair seats and furniture coverings embroidered in all over patterns like this one were very much in vogue in fashionable eighteenth-century American homes. The popularity of "needle-made" tapestries arose out of a desire to imitate the luxurious and expensive woven fabrics produced in Europe.

This cover must have adorned somebody's favorite chair, for the embroidery is badly worn. Fortunately, the area along the edge, which was turned under the seat, is perfectly preserved. I found the colors along this small strip so lively that I carefully cut away a section of the lining to inspect the back of the embroidery. Beautiful pinks, yellows, blues, reds, and corals emerged — brighter than I'd ever imagined.

(Above:) Queen Anne-style chair seat cover. Cross stitch embroidery on canvas in colored wools. 19¼ x 22¾ inches. American, eighteenth century. Gift of A. D. Compton, 1924. (Opposite: Adaptation mounted on a Queen Anne-style side chair (Philadelphia, about 1725–1750), from the Museum's American Wing. Rogers Fund, 1925.)

COLOR PLACEMENT CHART

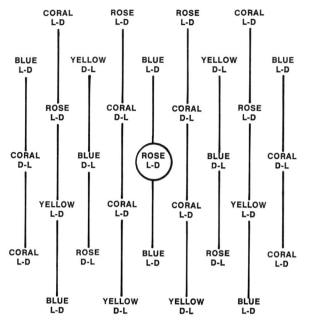

Finished size: A 14-inch square, worked on 11-mesh penelope canvas, produces a design of five horizontal rows of leaves, with three full leaves in Rows One, Three, and Five, and two full leaves in Rows Two and Four

Stitch: Cross

Materials: 11-mesh penelope canvas; three-strand Persian wool; #20 tapestry needle; one-inch masking tape; 4H pencil

Colors (numbers refer to Paternayan wool):

Yellow leaves	Blue leaves	Coral leaves	Rose leaves
010 White	010 White	010 White	010 White
427 Dk. Gold	334 Dk. Blue	R69 Red	231 Dk. Rose
440 Med. Gold	385 Med. Blue	R86 Coral	282 Med. Rose
442 Lt. Yellow	395 Lt. Blue	265 Lt. Coral	256 Lt. Rose

Colors for background and outline
050 Black
321 Dk. Blue
528 Dk. Green
527 Med. Green
Y50 Lt. Yellow/Green

Working instructions: (Color illustration page 25.)

If the pattern is being worked as a chair seat covering, then trace an outline of the finished shape on the canvas. (The selvage should be on the left.) Before cutting, be sure to allow for the thickness of the seat, the amount necessary for finishing (the edge to be turned under), and an extra two inches on all sides for blocking.

- Bind the raw edges of the canvas with masking tape. Locate the center of the canvas by folding it in half, then in quarters. Mark the center lines on double vertical and double horizontal threads, using a 4H pencil.

- Separate the three-strand wool and use a *single* strand throughout.

- Begin the stitching in the center of the canvas. First outline the central leaf in Black, then do the Black outline of the surrounding leaves.

- Fill in the individual leaf shapes, working from the outline toward the center. Begin with the White, then fill in the colors (see Color Placement Chart). The central section of each leaf is worked in three shades, ranging either from dark to light (D-L) or light to dark (L-D). The sides of the leaves are worked in two shades: dark and medium. If the central section is colored dark to light (from the outline toward the center of the shape), then work the side shapes from light to dark.

- Do the background last; begin with the Dk. Blue and end with the Lt. Yellow/Green.

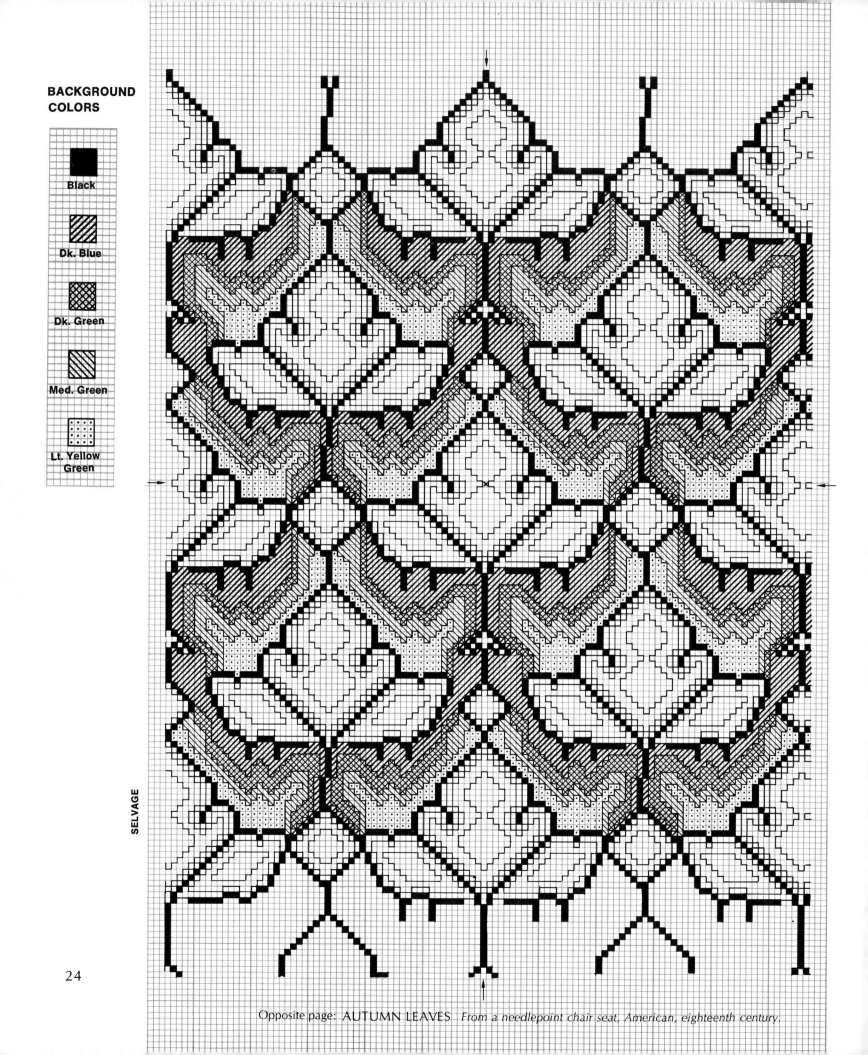

BACKGROUND COLORS

Black

Dk. Blue

Dk. Green

Med. Green

Lt. Yellow Green

SELVAGE

24

Opposite page: AUTUMN LEAVES   *From a needlepoint chair seat, American, eighteenth century.*

STILL LIFE WITH GRAPES *From a tapestry-woven decorative square, Egyptian (Coptic), probably fifth–sixth century* A.D.

Opposite page: RAINBOW GEOMETRIC *From a needlepoint sampler, probably Italian, dated 1760.*

PASTORAL LANDSCAPE   *From a needlepoint picture, American, about 1750.*

Opposite page: FANTASTIC FLOWERS   *From a crewel-embroidered hanging, French, eighteenth century.*

GRAPEVINES IN INTERLACING BANDS   *From a tapestry-woven ornament, Egyptian (Coptic), probably fourth century* A.D.

Opposite page: PAIR OF PEACOCKS   *From a crewel-embroidered bed hanging, English, late seventeenth century.*

SACRED LOTUS   *From an embroidered rank badge, Chinese, early nineteenth century.*

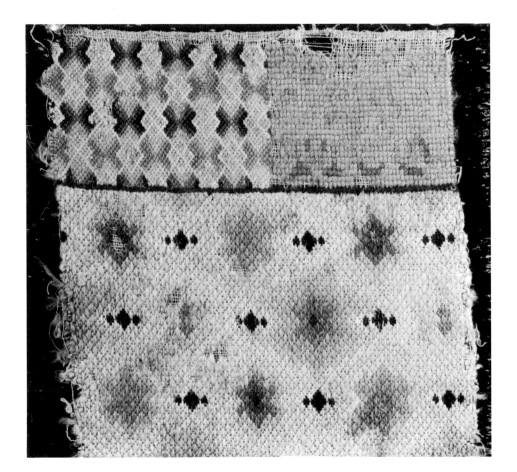

Fragment of a sampler. Hungarian Point and Tent stitch embroidery on coarse linen in colored wools. 8 ⅛ x 8 inches. Probably Italian, dated 1760. Gift of the United Piece Dye Works, 1936. (Adaptation of Tent stitch detail on following page.)

Rainbow Geometric

Designs like these are very reminiscent of the bold geometric patterns found on peasant costumes and embroideries from Eastern Europe. However, the colors — shades of yellow, blue, carnation, and pink — would indicate that this embroidery is Western European in origin. It is more than likely from Italy or was copied from an Italian pattern.

For at least three hundred years stitches like Florentine and Hungarian Point were used extensively throughout Europe. They probably originated out of a desire to emulate the textures of certain types of woven fabrics. The Italians perfected the stitches, creating embroideries with luminous and beautiful shaded effects whose appeal was not limited to Italy. Even today these designs remain a challenge to needleworkers, as evidenced by the many recent publications that include old Florentine embroidery patterns.

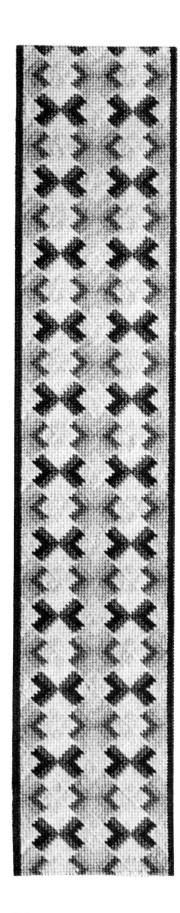

Finished size: 17½ x 20½ inches

Stitch: Hungarian Point

Materials: 13-mesh mono canvas, 25 x 22 inches; three-strand Persian wool; #18 tapestry needle; 4H pencil

Colors (numbers refer to Paternayan wool):

Yellows	*Corals*
442 Yellow, 55 full strands	265 Lt. Coral, 55 full strands
445 Lt. Ochre, 15 full strands	260 Med. Coral, 15 full strands
433 Dk. Ochre, 15 full strands	245 Dk. Coral, 15 full strands
Roses	*Blues*
281 Lt. Rose, 55 full strands	395 Lt. Blue, 47 full strands
275 Med. Rose, 20 full strands	385 Med. Blue, 20 full strands
234 Dk. Rose, 15 full strands	334 Dk. Blue, 15 full strands
Background	
010 White, 95 full strands	
105 Antique Black, 15 full strands	

Working instructions: (Color illustration page 27.)

Since this is a repeat pattern, the overall size of the finished embroidery is determined by the object to be covered. The design, colors, and texture suggest a covering for a strong accent piece, such as a side chair, footstool, or a large throw or floor pillow.

- Before cutting the canvas, be sure to measure carefully the object to be covered; allow additional canvas for any finishing necessary and add to that at least two inches on all sides for blocking.

- Bind the raw edges of the canvas with masking tape. Locate the center of the canvas by folding it in half, then in quarters. Mark the center lines, using a 4H pencil.

- Use the three-strand wool full strength throughout the embroidery.

- The entire piece is worked in Hungarian Point. The two short stitches cover two horizontal threads on the canvas, and the long stitch covers four horizontal threads (see stitch instructions for Hungarian Point).

- Begin the pattern in the center of the canvas. The central diamond motif is in shades of Rose. Start with the Lt. Rose color and work in horizontal rows of three-stitch units or use the alternate method suggested in the diagram. In the alternate method the stitches follow the zigzag outline of the pattern as if a Bargello design were being worked. The stitches are worked in groups of two; the third stitch is filled in on a separate return journey. This method minimizes canvas distortion, so little or no blocking is necessary upon completion. To locate the starting stitch, count 27 spaces on the canvas from the center line toward the right; then count up 5 spaces toward the top. Bring the needle out into this space for the first small stitch.

- Fill in each diamond shape, working colors from light to dark. Then fill in the White outline around the shape, and finally the small Black diamonds.

- Consult the color illustration for placement of the Yellow, Coral, Rose, and Blue diamonds.

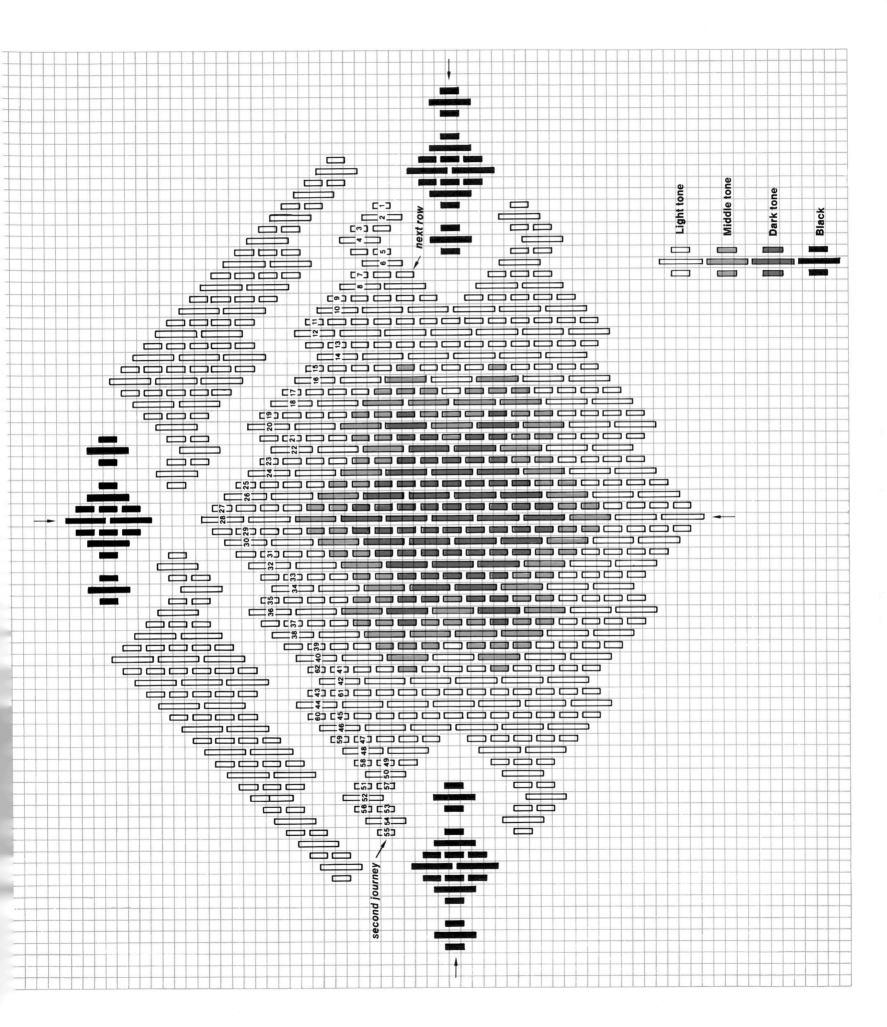

next row

second journey

Light tone

Middle tone

Dark tone

Black

Decorative square. Tapestry woven in colored wools and undyed linen.
10¼ x 10¼ inches. Egyptian (Coptic), probably fifth–sixth century A.D.
Gift of George F. Baker, 1890. (Detail opposite.)

The subject matter of this pattern has its roots in a popular Greco-Roman theme: the celebration of the powers of Bacchus, god of wine. Baskets of fruit, grapes, vines, and scenes of the pagan god — often shown in a drunken state — are recurring images in the art of the classical world. Here the basket of grapes is surrounded by a border of corner rosettes and budding lotuses.

Although a portion of the original weaving is worn away, it was relatively easy to reconstruct its design because of the characteristic symmetry of Coptic textiles.

Still Life with Grapes

Finished size: 16½ x 17 inches

Stitches: Tent and Diagonal Tent (Basket Weave)

Materials: 10-mesh mono canvas, 21 x 21 inches; three-strand Persian wool; #16 tapestry needle; one-inch masking tape

Colors (numbers refer to Paternayan wool):

020 Off White, 65 full strands	560 Lt. Green, 32 full strands
445 Gold, 80 full strands	516 Dk. Green, 20 full strands
265 Pink, 25 full strands	330 Blue, 20 full strands
R86 Coral, 60 full strands	416 Orange, 10 full strands
R69 Red, 10 full strands	115 Dk. Brown, 125 full strands

Working instructions: *(Color illustration page 26.)*

The design measures H. 168 mesh x W. 165 mesh. The 21-inch square canvas allows at least two inches all around for blocking.

- Bind the raw edges of the canvas with masking tape.

- Use the three-strand wool full strength throughout.

- The entire design may be worked in Tent stitch, or outline the shapes in Tent and fill in the larger areas in Diagonal Tent. The wool quantities given are sufficient for either method.

- Begin the pattern in the upper right corner. Mark a point on the canvas two inches down from the top and two inches in from the right side; this intersection corresponds to the corner mesh of the design and the square in the upper right corner on the chart.

- The easiest way to work the pattern is to outline the shapes first, then fill in the centers. Do the background areas last.

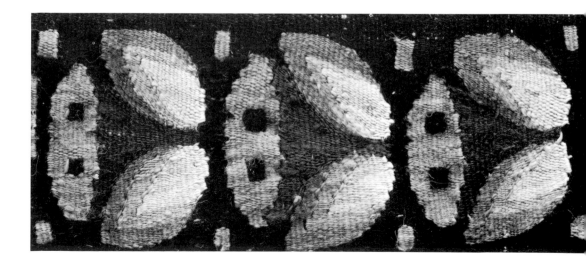

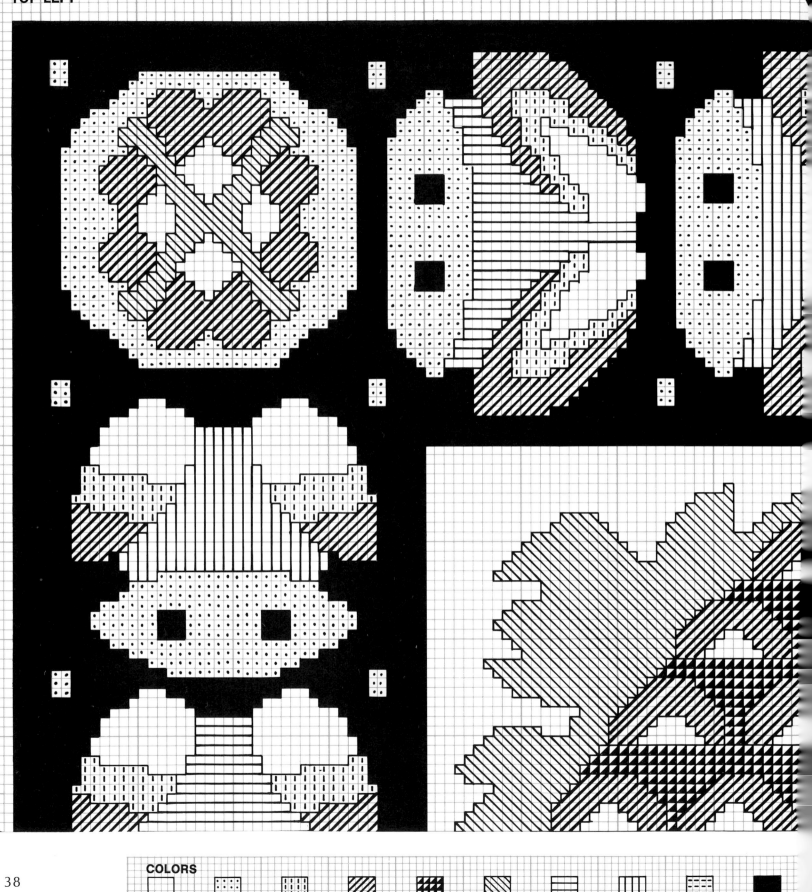

COLORS

Off White | Gold | Pink | Coral | Red | Lt. Green | Dk. Green | Blue | Orange | Dk. Brown

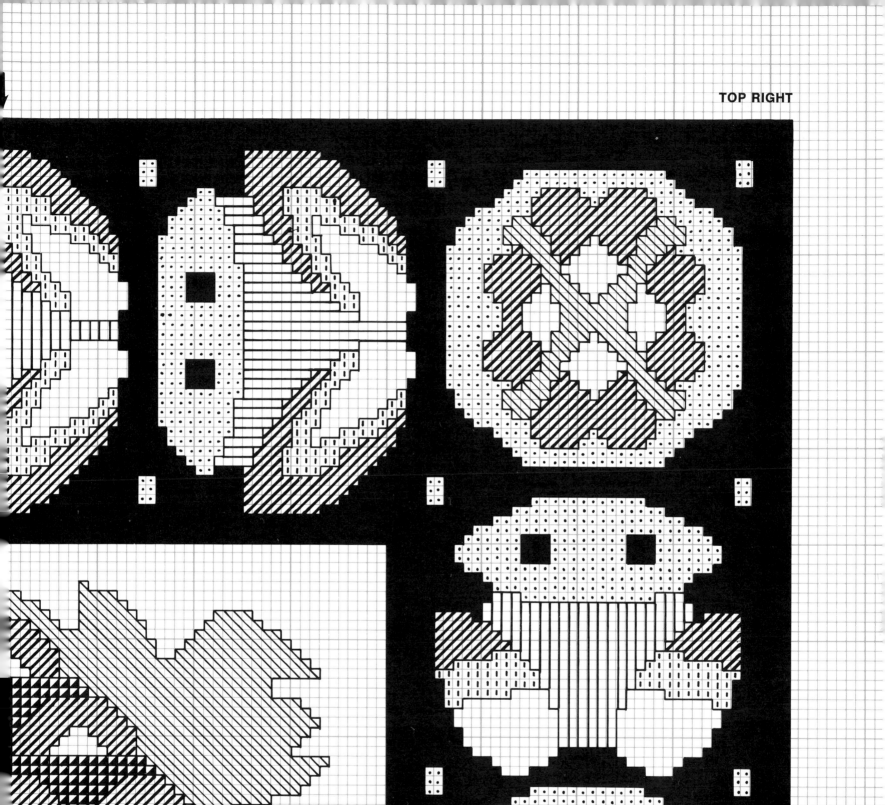

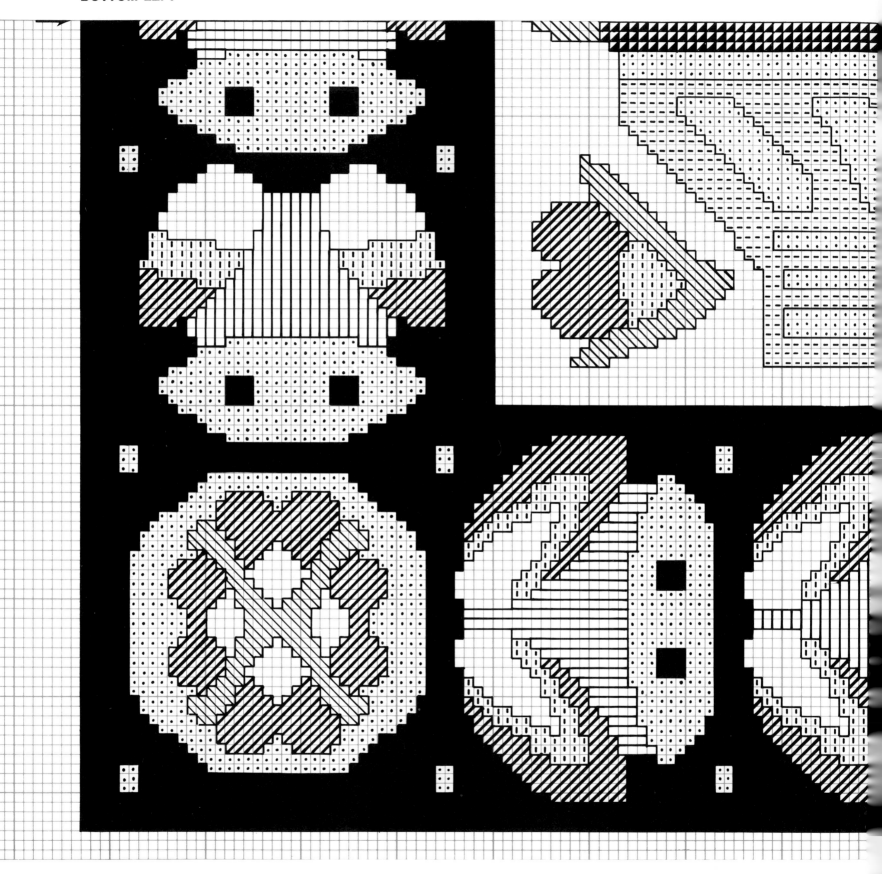

COLORS

| Off White | Gold | Pink | Coral | Red | Lt. Green | Dk. Green | Blue | Orange | Dk. Brown |

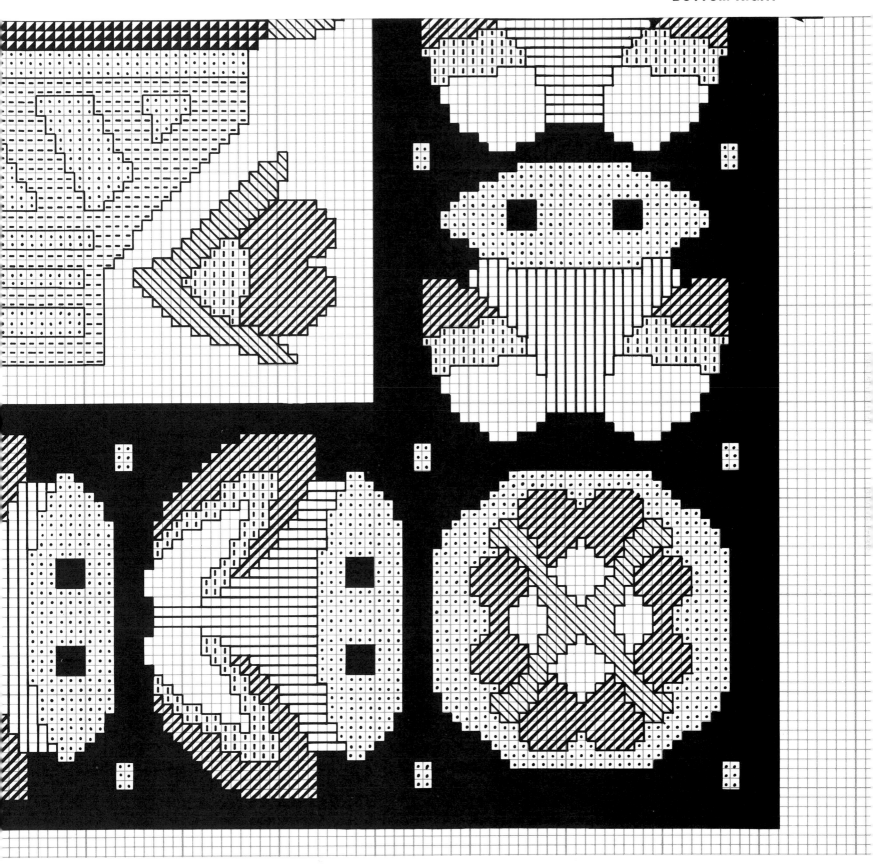

Hanging. Crewel embroidery on linen, worked in Long-and-Short, Satin, Stem, and Chain stitches and French Knots. 68 x 60½ inches. French, 1735–1775 (period of Louis XV). Rogers Fund, 1944. (Details above and opposite.)

Fantastic Flowers

The sumptuary laws passed in France in the late seventeenth century to protect domestic industries did little to lessen the French taste for fabrics *indiennes*. In spite of edicts prohibiting the importation of Indian textiles and the copying of Indian designs by French manufacturers, the fashion for these exotic and brightly colored designs seemed to increase. Printed and painted cottons and beautiful Kashmir shawls were smuggled into the country, and French textile manufacturers carried on their illegal operations secretly under the most threatening conditions.

Well into the eighteenth century embroidery designs were greatly influenced by Eastern patterns. During the period of Louis XV, bold floral designs, colored in bright scarlets, yellows, blues, and greens, prevailed. The exotic flora of India — the mangrove, poppy, tulip, pomegranate, chrysanthemum, rose peony, and magnolia — were redrawn and "westernized" to suit the French taste.

Finished size: The embroidered area measures 8¾ x 10 inches
Stitches: Long-and-Short, Satin, Stem, Chain, and French Knot
Materials: Natural-colored linen twill; three-strand Persian wool; #18 tapestry needle; tracing paper; blue dressmaker's carbon; artists' stretchers
Colors (numbers refer to Paternayan wool):

365 Dk. Blue, 3 full strands	845 Red, 2 full strands
330 Med. Blue, 1 full strand	860 Pink, 1 full strand
386 Lt. Blue, 2 full strands	457 Yellow, 5 full strands
396 Pale Blue, 2 full strands	438 Lt. Yellow, 1 full strand
504 Dk. Green, 5 full strands	427 Gold, 2 full strands
527 Med. Green, 4 full strands	050 Black, 1 full strand

Working instructions: (Color illustration page 28.)

- Enlarge the design and copy on tracing paper. Transfer the pattern to the fabric using dressmaker's carbon.

- Mount the fabric on the artists' stretchers.

- Use a *single* strand of the three-strand wool throughout.

- Consult the Stitch and Color Chart for placement of colors, stitches, and direction of stitches.

enlarge to 10"

STITCH AND COLOR CHART

COLORS		STITCHES	
1	Dk. Blue	Long-and-Short	
2	Med. Blue	Satin	
3	Lt. Blue	Stem	
4	Pale Blue	Chain	
5	Dk. Green	French Knot	
6	Med. Green		
7	Red		
8	Pink		
9	Yellow		
10	Lt. Yellow		
11	Gold		
12	Black		

45

Pastoral Landscape

Needlepoint pastoral scenes were popular in England throughout the eighteenth century, and this American "woolen picture" is in that tradition. The subjects, however, were probably daily events in the embroiderer's own life. The scene, drawn with a certain naïveté and primitiveness, is idyllic, yet the costumes and activities are typical of a colonial autumn day. Set against a backdrop of rolling hillocks, the shepherd plays his pipe and a playful dog prances to the tune, while sheep flock to his side. The maiden gathers apples, wild geese fly through the clouds overhead, and below, ducks and ducklings wade in a shallow pool.

Needlepoint picture on canvas in colored wools. Embroidered in petit point (Tent stitch). 16¾ x 17½ inches. American, about 1750. Pulitzer Fund, 1939. (Detail opposite.)

Finished size: 18 x 17½ inches

Stitches: Tent and Diagonal Tent (Basket Weave)

Materials: 10-mesh mono canvas, 22 x 22 inches; three-strand Persian wool; #16 tapestry needle; one-inch masking tape

Colors (numbers refer to Paternayan Persian wool):

334 Dk. Blue, 60 full strands	250 Dk. Rose, 8 full strands
385 Med. Blue, 55 full strands	254 Lt. Rose, 8 full strands
395 Lt. Blue, 10 full strands	275 Med. Pink, 12 full strands
104 Dk. Brown, 35 full strands	563 Lt. Yellow/Green, 48 full strands
462 Med. Brown, 45 full strands	352 Lt. Blue/Green, 45 full strands
492 Beige, 25 full strands	010 White, 155 full strands

Working instructions: (Color illustration page 29.)

The design measures H. 176 x W. 180 mesh. The 22 x 22–inch canvas allows two inches on all sides for blocking.

- Bind the raw edges of the canvas with masking tape.

- Use the three-strand wool full strength throughout the embroidery. Since many of the wools are close in color, keep them clearly marked and separated as you work.

- You may work the entire design in Tent stitch, or outline the shapes in Tent and fill in the larger areas in Diagonal Tent. The wool quantities given are sufficient for either method.

- Begin the pattern in the upper right corner. For proper placement of the design, mark a point two inches down from the top and two inches in from the right side of the canvas; this intersection corresponds to the square in the upper right corner of the chart.

- Work a small section of the background, then outline the leaves on the tree. Continue to outline the shapes, then fill in the centers as you go along. Fill in the background after the scene is completely embroidered.

COLORS

| Dk. Blue | Med. Blue | Lt. Blue | Dk. Brown | Med. Brown | Beige | Dk. Rose | Lt. Rose | Med. Pink | Lt. Yellow/ Green | Lt. Blue/ Green | White |

BOTTOM LEFT

COLORS

| Dk. Blue | Med. Blue | Lt. Blue | Dk. Brown | Med. Brown | Beige | Dk. Rose | Lt. Rose | Med. Pink | Lt. Yellow/Green | Lt. Blue/Green | White |

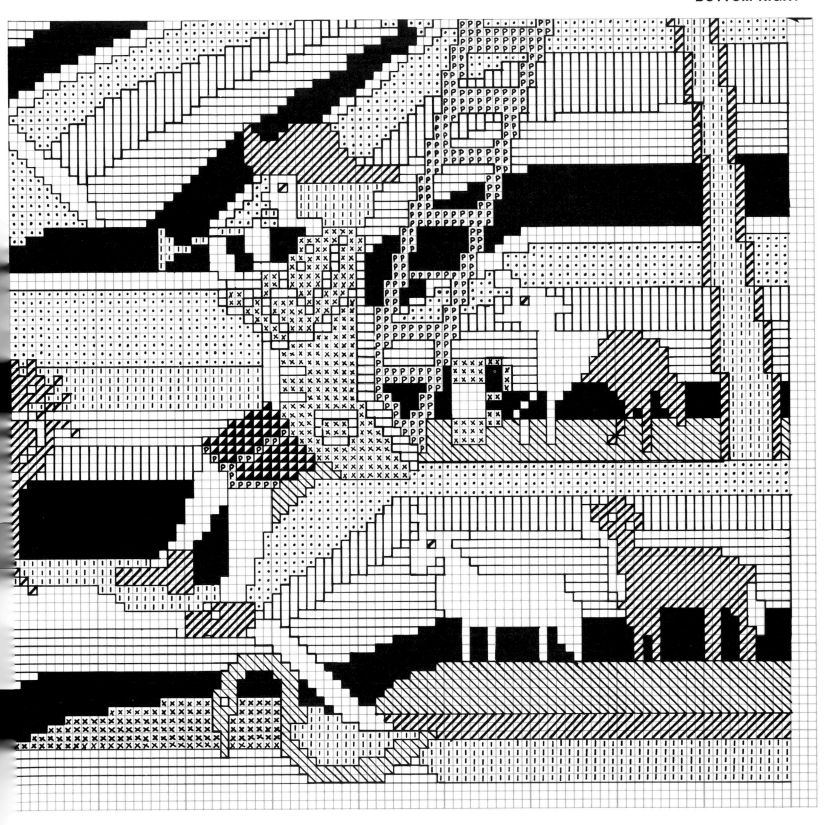

Ornamental design from a Coptic tunic. Tapestry woven in deep blue-purple wool and undyed linen. 6 ½ x 5 ⅞ inches. Egyptian, probably fourth century A.D. Purchase, Subscription Fund, 1889. (Detail opposite.)

During the period Egypt was dominated by the Roman and Byzantine empires, the principal mode of dress for Egyptians of both sexes was the tunic. The front and back of the tunic were decorated with woven ornamental bands circling the shoulders, neck, and hem. Square designs like this one usually appeared along the shoulders and hem.

The Copts (members of the early Christian church of Egypt) incorporated many classical themes and motifs in their designs; the grapevine and interlacing bands, often found in Roman mosaics and architectural decoration, are typical. This design may conceal a Byzantine cross formed on the white ground by the dark pattern of grape leaves — if you squint, you can see it.

Grapevines in Interlacing Bands

Finished size: 14 x 14 inches

Stitches: Tent and Diagonal Tent (Basket Weave)

Materials: 13-mesh mono canvas, 18 x 18 inches; three-strand Persian wool; #20 tapestry needle; one-inch masking tape

Colors (numbers refer to Paternayan Persian wool):
010 White, 115 full strands
365 Blue, 140 full strands

Working instructions: (Color illustration page 30.)

The sample measures 185 x 185 mesh; the 18-inch square canvas allows an additional two inches on all sides for blocking.

- Bind the raw edges of the canvas with masking tape.

- Separate the three-strand wool and use *two* strands throughout.

- You may work the entire design in Tent stitch, or outline the shapes in Tent and fill in the larger areas in Diagonal Tent. The wool quantities given are sufficient for either method.

- Begin the pattern in the upper right corner. Mark a point two inches down from the top edge and two inches in from the right side; this intersection corresponds to the corner mesh of the design and the square in the upper right corner on the chart. (The chart shows only the upper half of the pattern.)

- Work a section of the outer border in White, then fill in the Blue areas.

- Go on to the interlaced border. Work the White areas first, then fill in the Blue areas. Count the corners *very carefully*, as the length of the band varies as it turns each corner.

- For the central design, work the Blue areas first, then fill in the White.

- When the area shown on the chart is complete, turn the chart upside down and finish the pattern.

COLORS

White

Blue

Crewel-embroidered bed hanging with a ''Tree of Life'' design, worked on linen twill in Brick, Stem, Long-and-Short, and Satin stitches, with accents in French and Bullion Knots. 7 feet 4 inches x 5 feet 5 inches. English, late seventeenth century. Rogers Fund, 1908. (Detail of two peacocks opposite.)

Pair of Peacocks

It wasn't until the eighteenth century that the ordinary English home included a separate bedroom; prior to this the bed was set up in any room of the house — sometimes even in the kitchen.

This elaborately embroidered hanging suggests the importance attached to bed decoration in the seventeenth century, for at that time the bed constituted the only real comfort in home furnishings. Outfitted with richly decorated curtains, coverlet, pillows, and valances, the bed provided warmth and privacy as well as a declaration of wealth and prestige.

The "Tree of Life" motif was one of the most popular designs in crewelwork of this period. In this embroidery, the tree is a large palm with mushroomlike leaves. The background is filled with exotic flowers, phoenixes, parrots, and peacocks. Elephants, cranes, and monkeys roam among the rolling hillocks in the foreground. The adaptation is of the two peacocks in the right foreground.

Finished size: The outline of the design measures 16 x 14 inches
Stitches: Stem, Brick, Long-and-Short, Satin, French and Bullion Knot
Materials: Natural-colored linen twill, 24 x 21 inches; three-strand Persian wool; #16 tapestry needle; tracing paper; blue dressmaker's carbon; artists' stretchers, 20 x 17 inches
Colors (numbers refer to Paternayan wool):

563 Lt. Yellow/Green, 7 full strands	386 Lt. Blue, 3 full strands
594 Med. Yellow/Green, 5 full strands	513 Off White, 23 full strands
546 Med. Green, 11 full strands	131 Brown, 12 full strands
314 Dk. Blue/Gray, 18 full strands	289 Pink, 13 full strands
342 Blue/Green, 9 full strands	280 Salmon, 4 full strands
365 Dk. Navy Blue, 8 full strands	

Working instructions: (Color illustration page 31.)

- Enlarge the design and copy on tracing paper. Transfer the pattern to the fabric using dressmaker's carbon; do not transfer the outline of the design.

- Mount the fabric on the artists' stretchers.

- Separate the three-strand wool and use *one* strand throughout.

- Work stitches in Satin, Long-and-Short, and Bullion using a single strand; for Stem, Brick, and French Knots use one strand doubled over to obtain a two-strand thickness (two separate strands will not pass through the fabric easily.) Keep the wools clearly marked and separated, as many of them are very close in hue.

- Since the design is done in a variety of stitches, different areas may be worked simultaneously to avoid tiring of a particular stitch. The only areas where the order of working is important are those done in Bullion Knots. Making these knots might upset the nearby stitches, so be sure to do the knots first, then fill in the surrounding areas.

PATTERN

enlarge to 14"

STITCH AND COLOR CHART

COLORS

1 Lt. Yellow/Green
2 Med. Yellow/Green
3 Med. Green
4 Dk. Blue/Gray
5 Blue/Green
6 Dk. Navy Blue
7 Lt. Blue
8 Off White
9 Brown
10 Pink
11 Salmon

STITCHES

Stem   A
Brick   B
Long-and-Short   C
Satin   D
French Knot   E
Bullion Knot   F

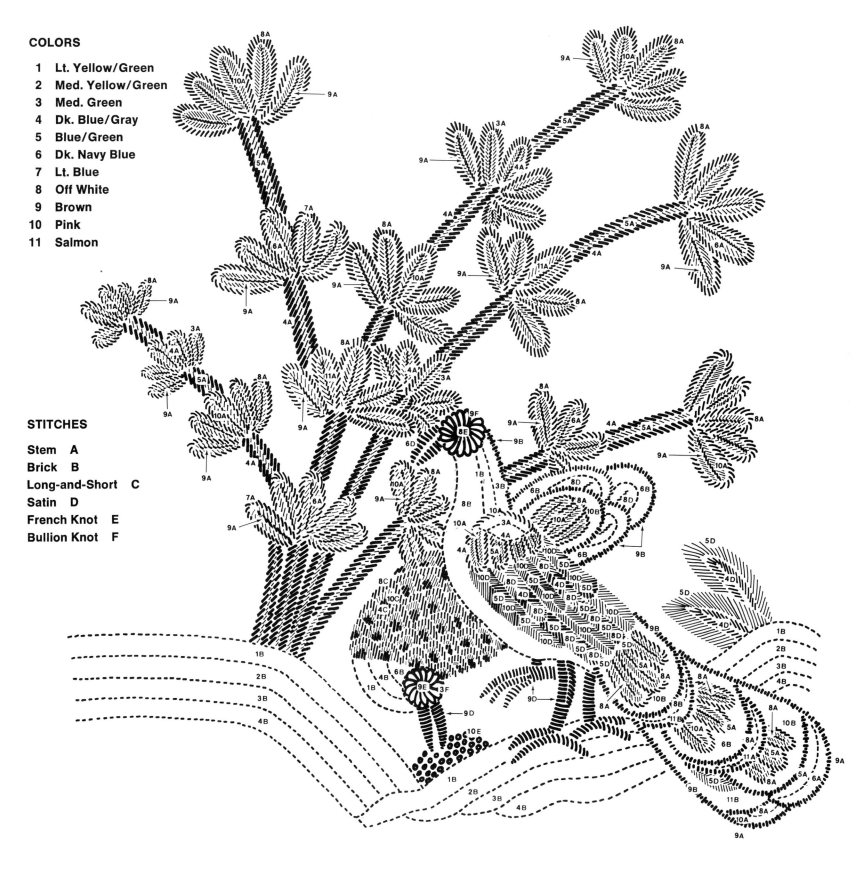

59

Rank badge from a costume belonging to a civil official of the First Rank.
Petit point embroidery (Tent stitch) on silk gauze in colored silk threads.
10½ x 11 inches. Chinese, Ch'ing dynasty, early nineteenth century.
Bequest of William Christian Paul, 1930. (Detail above; badge opposite.)

Rank badges were worn by dignitaries of the Chinese court from the Ming dynasty (1368–1644) until the end of the last imperial dynasty (Ch'ing dynasty, 1644–1911). These insignia were prominantly placed on the chest and back of robes and jackets reserved for official functions, making the wearer's rank immediately evident. Most of these badges were made in shops by men and boys with, as one author describes them, "strong fingers."

Sacred Lotus

The badge illustrated contains a Manchurian crane, which not only indicated rank, but conveyed the sentiment of long life to the wearer, since according to Chinese legend the crane was supposed to live for hundreds of years. The background is decorated with auspicious lotus flowers and other Buddhist symbols. The needlepoint adaptation is of a motif from the background; it includes lotus flowers (symbols of purity and enlightenment) entwined with foliated scrolls which represent sacred rays. The wheellike central motif of flowers represents the perpetual cycles of existence.

Finished size: 15¼ x 15¼ inches
Stitches: Tent and Diagonal Tent (Basket Weave)
Materials: 13-mesh mono canvas, 19½ x 19½ inches; three-strand Persian wool;
   #20 tapestry needle; one-inch masking tape; 4H pencil
Colors (numbers refer to Paternayan wool):

005 White, 10 full strands	555 Green, 35 full strands
425 Peach, 140 full strands	207 Burgundy, 10 full strands
756 Lt. Blue, 35 full strands	350 Med. Blue, 45 full strands
Y44 Yellow, 25 full strands	304 Dk. Blue, 20 full strands

Working instructions: (Color illustration page 32.)
The design measures 200 x 200 mesh. The 19½-inch square canvas allows two extra inches on all sides for blocking.

- Bind the raw edges of the canvas with masking tape. Locate the center of the canvas by folding it in half, then in quarters. Mark the center lines, using a 4H pencil.

- Separate the three-strand wool and use *two* strands throughout.

- The entire design may be stitched in Tent, or outline the shapes in Tent and fill in the larger areas in Diagonal Tent. The wool quantities given are sufficient for either method.

- To begin, work all the Yellow framework, counting carefully. When the Yellow outlines on the top half are complete, turn the graph upside down and complete the lower half.

- Next, stitch the Green areas between the Yellow lines of the framework, then the Lt. Blue areas between the Yellow lines.

- Fill in the central wheel of flowers; work the Dk. Blue outlines first, then fill in the centers. Complete the Green background.

- Next, do the Green and Lt. Blue lotus flowers in each segment; work the outlines first, then fill in the centers. Do the foliated scrolls, then fill in the Peach background.

- Stitch the diaper-patterned background last, beginning in the upper right corner. Do the Med. Blue outlines first, then fill in the Peach background. Note that at the center on all four sides only *half* a repeat of the Med. Blue diaper pattern appears.

COLORS

| Dk. Blue | Med. Blue | Burgundy | Green | Yellow | Lt. Blue | Peach | White |

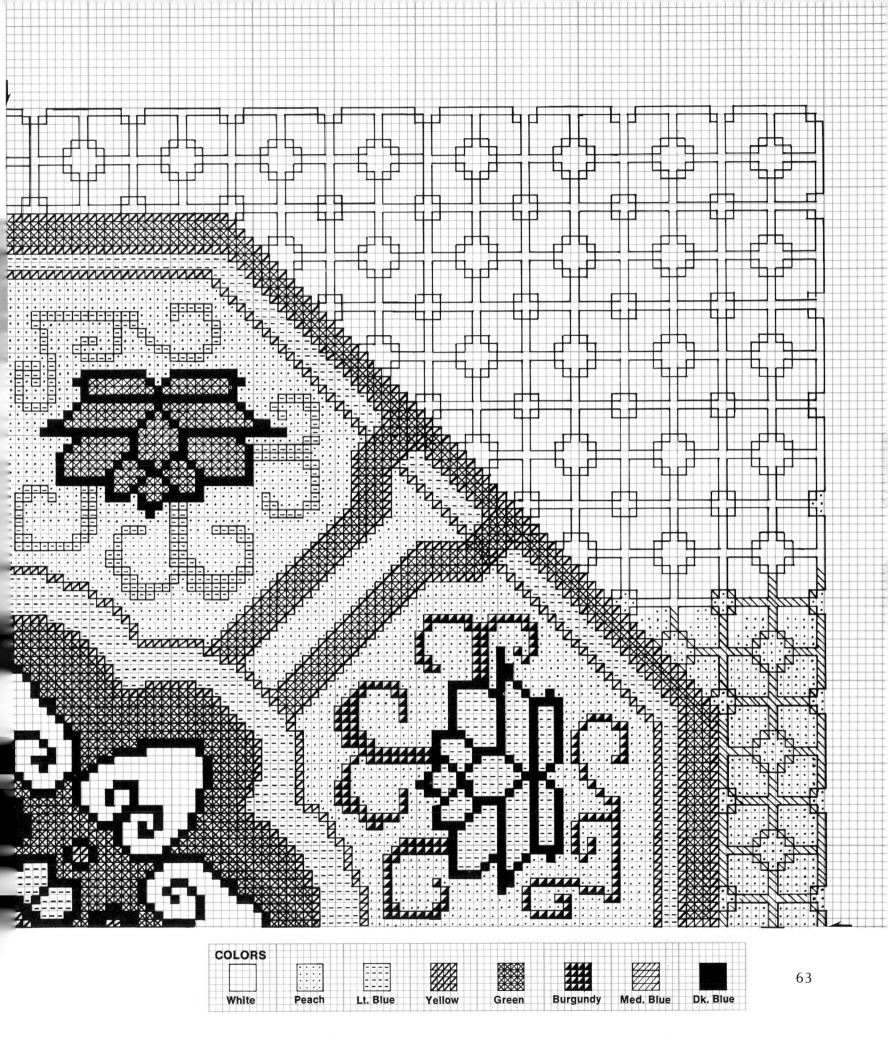

COLORS

White	Peach	Lt. Blue	Yellow	Green	Burgundy	Med. Blue	Dk. Blue

63

Panel, possibly part of a larger piece. Florentine stitch embroidery on silk gauze in colored silk threads. 11 x 11 inches. Chinese, late Ming dynasty, seventeenth century. Gift of Miss Ellen Barker, 1942. (Detail above; complete panel opposite.)

By the time of the Ming dynasty, Chinese embroidery had a history of some three thousand years, yet it wasn't until this late stage that stitches like Florentine and Tent began to appear. Like the one illustrated, most Chinese counted-thread designs were embroidered on silk gauze — a lightweight, open-weave fabric that was commonly used for summer costumes.

The embroidery portrays an idyllic scene along the banks of a meandering river. In it we find boat houses on stilts, a covered bridge, a small fishing boat, decorative rocks and richly foliated evergreens and flowering trees. The stylized treatment of the trees is particularly interesting, and no two are alike. The various symbols — the arrows, crosses, circles, triangles — are used for the foliage to differentiate types. All of the neatly arranged elements are united by the red-colored water. Red was used symbolically by the Chinese to connote joy and happiness, and was sometimes associated with marriage.

Along the River Bank

Finished size: 12¼ x 13½ inches

Stitches: Tent and Diagonal Tent (Basket Weave)

Materials: 13-mesh mono canvas, 17 x 18 inches; three-strand Persian wool; #20 tapestry needle; one-inch masking tape

Colors (numbers refer to Paternayan wool):

R80 Red, 68 full strands	516 Dk. Green, 23 full strands
496 Off White, 18 full strands	145 Brown, 12 full strands
166 Gray, 15 full strands	395 Lt. Blue, 25 full strands
531 Gold, 15 full strands	385 Med. Blue, 22 full strands
546 Lt. Green, 10 full strands	334 Dk. Blue, 15 full strands
560 Med. Green, 18 full strands	108 Charcoal Black, 6 full strands

Working instructions: *(Color illustration page 74.)*

The design measures H. 160 x W. 180 mesh. The 17 x 18–inch canvas allows at least two inches on all sides for blocking.

- Bind the raw edges of the canvas with masking tape.

- Separate the three-strand wool and use *two* strands throughout.

- The entire design may be worked in Tent stitch, or outline the shapes in Tent and fill in the larger areas in Diagonal Tent. The yarn quantities given are sufficient for either method.

- Begin the pattern in the upper right corner. For proper placement of the design on the canvas, mark a point two inches down from the top and two inches in from the right side; this intersection corresponds to the corner mesh of the design and the square in the upper right corner on the chart. Follow the charted graph for the design and the placement of the colors. The background should be filled in after the scene is completed.

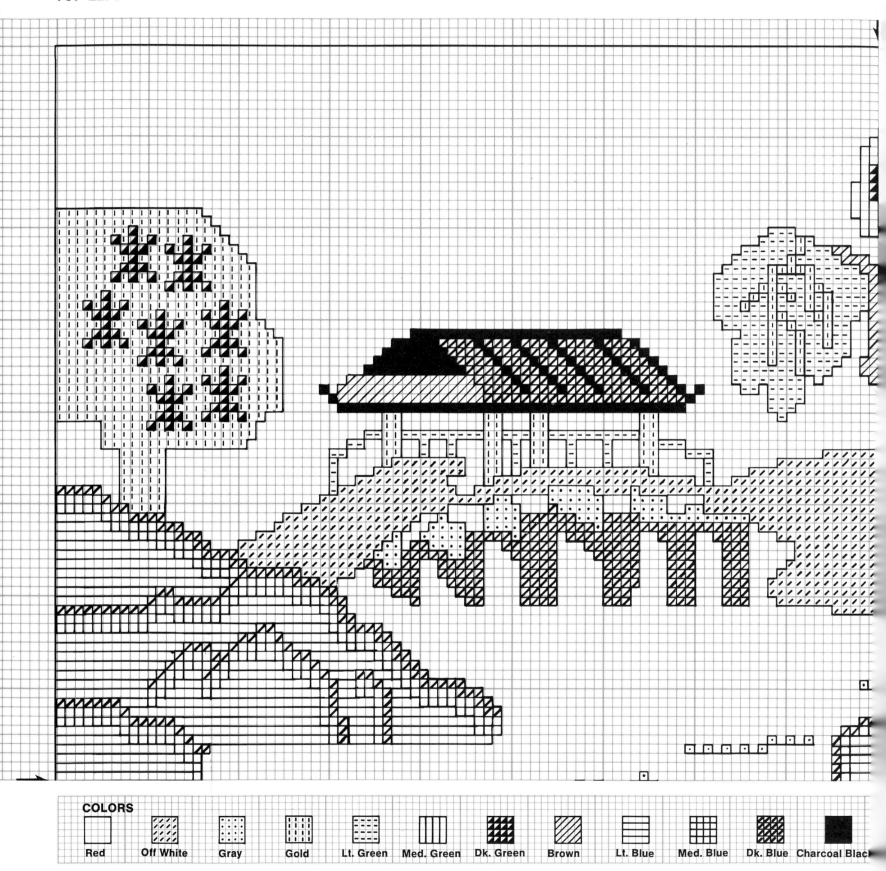

COLORS

| Red | Off White | Gray | Gold | Lt. Green | Med. Green | Dk. Green | Brown | Lt. Blue | Med. Blue | Dk. Blue | Charcoal Black |

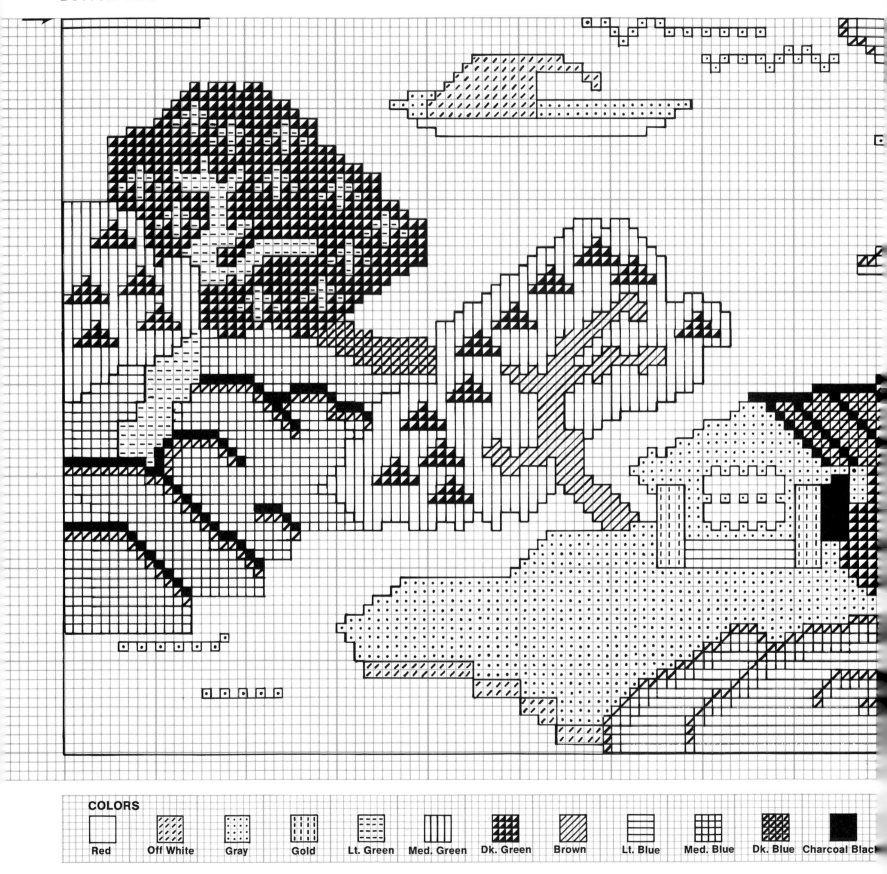

COLORS

| Red | Off White | Gray | Gold | Lt. Green | Med. Green | Dk. Green | Brown | Lt. Blue | Med. Blue | Dk. Blue | Charcoal | Black |

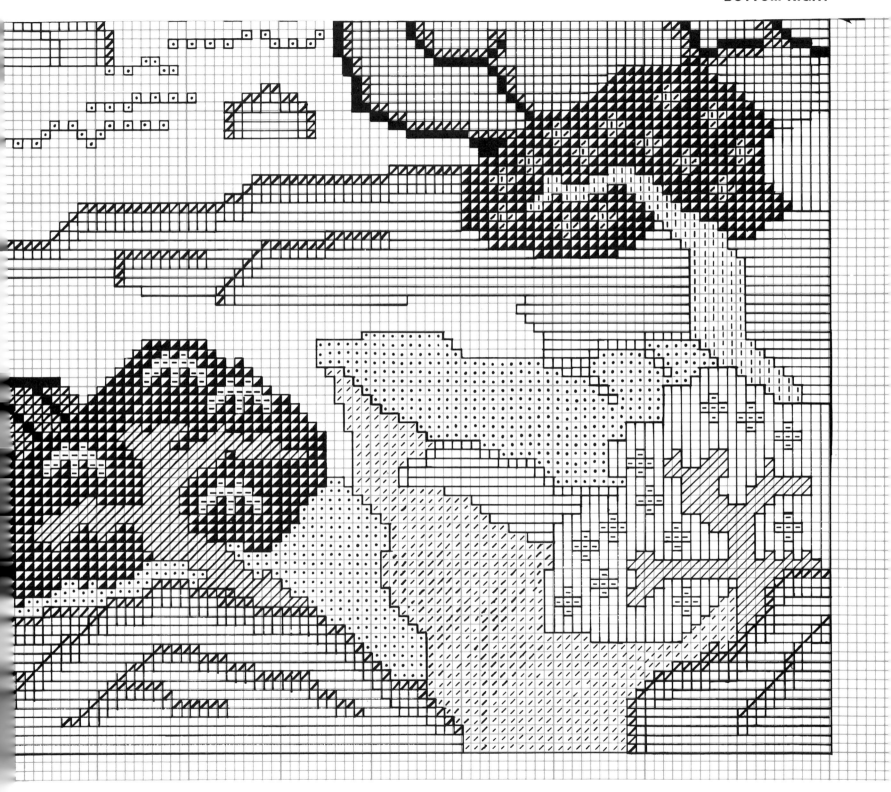

Sampler. Embroidery on linen canvas in silk and silver threads. Stitched in Gobelin, Tent, Chain, Cross, Plait, and Rococo. 16¼ x 10⅜ inches. English, first half of the seventeenth century. From the Collection of Mrs. Lathrop Colgate Harper, Bequest, 1957. (Detail above; complete sampler opposite.)

Much of the English domestic embroidery surviving from the seventeenth century was the work of young girls, and a girl's training in needlework began with the sampler. Here was the place to practice and try out new stitches; this knowledge might later be applied to more ambitious projects, such as the decoration of clothing or bed hangings.

The sampler shown is filled with floral and geometric motifs worked in a variety of stitches. Among them is the thistle pattern in Rococo stitch which inspired my adaptation. It is curious that this beautiful stitch was not more frequently used; it appears mostly in English embroideries. Needle-made lace and drawn-thread work were very popular in England at this time, as were delicately embroidered undergarments. Rococo stitch may have been inspired by this fashion for open-work and fragile embroideries since the characteristic holes, left in the canvas, create a very lacey effect.

$\mathcal{F}$lowering $\mathcal{T}$histle

Finished size: 13 x 13 inches
Stitch: Rococo
Materials: 13-mesh mono canvas, 17 x 17 inches; six-strand mercerized cotton;
    #20 tapestry needle; one-inch masking tape
Colors (numbers refer to D.M.C. cotton):

351 Red, 4 skeins	320 Green, 4 skeins
758 Pink, 3 skeins	Ecru, 28 skeins

Working instructions: *(Color illustration page 73.)*

Since this is a central-motif design, the overall size is determined by the object to be covered. The central motif measures H. 117 x W. 114 mesh. The sample was designed to cover a 13-inch square pillow, and in this case the overall finished size measures 174 x 180 mesh. The pattern would also be lovely on a handbag or a book cover.

- Bind the raw edges of the canvas with masking tape.

- Work the entire design in Rococo stitch using all six strands (full strength) of the mercerized cotton throughout. Keep the threads smooth and untwisted as they are worked.

- To place the design on the canvas, mark a point two inches down from the top and two inches in from the right side; this intersection corresponds to the mesh in the upper right corner of the finished background.

- Work the Red area on the top flower first. Before beginning the embroidery enlarge the holes in the canvas in diamond shapes within the Red area (see instructions for Rococo stitch and the charted graph). To place the flower on the canvas, count in 63 mesh from the right corner mesh along the top, then down 27 mesh. Enlarge the first hole directly below and to the left of this mesh. This hole will become the top point of the first Rococo stitch.

- After completing the Red area, enlarge the holes on the canvas for the stitches in the Pink center of the top flower; fill in the stitches.

- Complete the Green areas next in the same way.

- Note the direction of the stitches on the four large side buds; some of these stitches are worked so that they appear horizontal. In the solid Red buds a combination of vertical and horizontal stitches is used within the same bud. The direction of the lettering on the charted graph indicates the position of the stitches in relation to the top edge of the canvas. Also note where half stitches are used in the stems and buds.

- Fill in the Ecru background last. Work the background from the design out toward the edges. Complete the edges on the right and left sides with vertical half stitches and the edges top and bottom with horizontal half stitches. (See color illustration for finishing of the top and bottom edges.)

Stitch One

COLORS

Red R

Pink P

Green G

Ecru background

FLOWERING THISTLE   *From an embroidered sampler, English, first half of the seventeenth century.*

ALONG THE RIVER BANK   *From an embroidered silk panel, Chinese, late Ming dynasty, seventeenth century.*

Opposite page: INDIANS IN FEATHERED HEADDRESSES   *From a loop-stitch embroidery, Peruvian, Late Chimu Culture, A.D. 1100–1400.*

CRICKET ON A CHINESE CABBAGE   *From an embroidered needle case, Chinese, nineteenth century.*

CHINESE MOSAIC   *From an embroidered fan case, Chinese, eighteenth–nineteenth century.*

PUPPIES   *From a tambour-embroidered carpet, American, dated 1835.*

KITTENS   *From a tambour-embroidered carpet, American, dated 1835.*   79

EARTH-COLORED PEASANT REPEAT   *From a peasant costume, Albanian or Montenegrin, eighteenth–nineteenth century.*

Indians in Feathered Headdresses

The descriptive treatment of the Indian heads in this embroidery provides us with an interesting document on the head and neck gear worn by the Peruvians prior to the Spanish conquest. A narrow headband worn over the forehead and fastened from behind with a cord is decorated with colorful feathers arranged in a semicircular fashion like symbolic rays. Ear plugs hung with decorative ornaments and feathers are attached to either side of the headdress. A feathered neckguard is worn around the neck. The faces of the Indians seem to be masked or painted — which would explain the color variations and their rather childlike appearance. One can only speculate whether these are warriors, priests, or even representations of a god, but the highly ornamental character of the headdress would suggest that this fragment was part of a ceremonial costume.

The original embroidery is worked in Vertical Loop stitch, which resembles Chain in appearance. The Peruvian's needle was improvised from a cactus thorn, and his finely spun wools were from the alpaca, llama, guanaco, and vicuna — animals indigenous to the Andean highlands.

Fragment. Peruvian Loop stitch embroidery in colored wools on brownish red cotton cloth. 15 ¼ x 13 inches. Peruvian (Central or South Coast), A.D. 1100–1400 (Late Chimu Culture). Gift of George D. Pratt, 1933. (Detail below; fragment on following page.)

Finished size: The sample measures 15 x 15 inches
Stitches: Chain and Split
Materials: Dark brown linen, 22 x 22 inches; three-strand Persian wool; #4 crewel needle; white dressmaker's carbon; tracing paper; artists' stretchers, 18 x 18 inches
Colors (numbers refer to Paternayan wool):

050 Black, 1 full strand	262 Red/Brown, 2 full strands
010 White, 2 full strands	350 Blue, 2 full strands
445 Ochre, 17 full strands	528 Green, 2 full strands
845 Red, 10 full strands	

Working instructions: (Color illustration page 75.)
The sample was designed to cover a pillow (15 inches square), but the pattern would also make a lively decoration for a child's coverlet or clothing.

- Enlarge the motif photostatically. Trace it as many times as necessary to fill the chosen area. Cut out the individual traced motifs and arrange them in the desired pattern. Tape them in place and retrace the pattern as laid out.

- Transfer the design to the fabric using white dressmaker's carbon. (If the line doesn't show up well, go over it with a white pencil.)

- Mount the fabric on artists' stretchers.

- Separate the three-strand wool and use a *single* strand throughout.

- The embroidery is worked in two easy stitches: Chain and Split. Work the Chain stitches approximately 5 to the inch and the Split stitches 8 to the inch. Consult the chart for placement of colors.

- To begin, embroider the area within the outlines of the face; then do the outline around the face and fill in the nose. Next, do the centers of the eyes; then outline them. Fill in the mouth. Complete the White lines on the mouth in Split stitch worked over the Chain stitches. Then do the headdress, earplugs, and neckguard. Fill in the centers first, then work a neat outline around each shape.

PATTERN

enlarge to 5¼"

COLOR CHART

1 **Black**
2 **White**
3 **Ochre**
4 **Red**
5 **Red/Brown**
6 **Blue**
7 **Green**

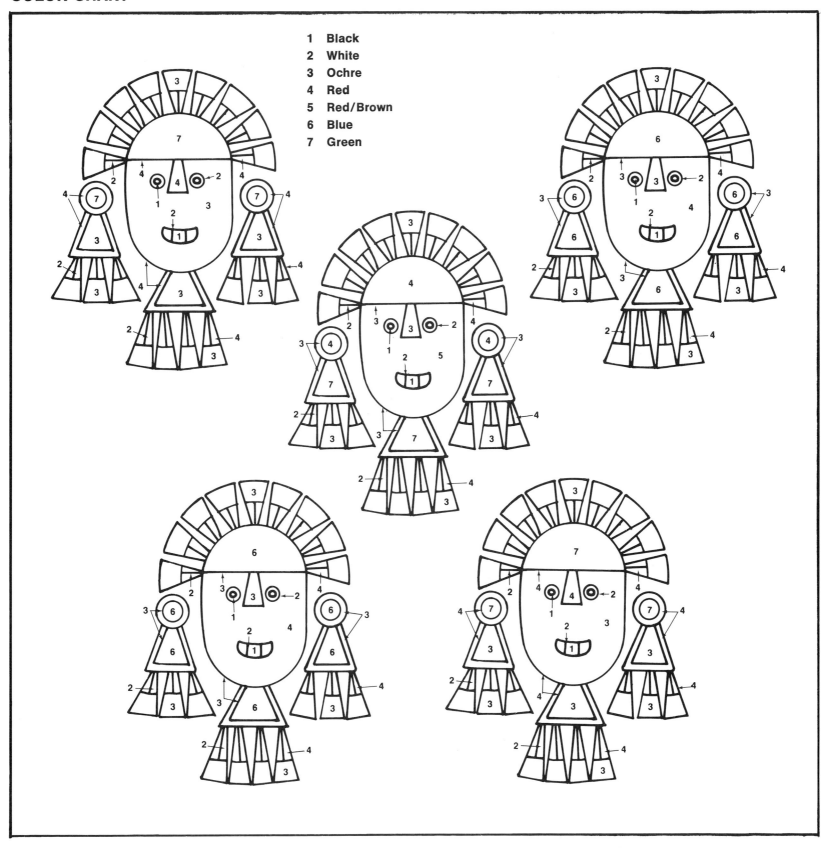

Needle case with a mirror on the reverse. Embroidery in couched silk braid on black satin. 3½ x 2⅝ inches. Chinese, nineteenth century. Gift of Florance Waterbury, 1944. (Detail above; needle case opposite.)

Cricket on a Chinese Cabbage

The cricket was treasured in imperial China for its beautiful "singing." Cricket fanciers were fastidious about selecting the right specimens for breeding and spent long hours nurturing the chosen insects and cultivating their voices. The prized crickets were placed in cages, usually made from gourds that had been specially molded into shapes offering the best acoustics. In the Metropolitan's collections there are cricket cages with elaborately carved jade and ivory covers that are valuable works of art.

This cricket is of the common vegetable-garden variety. He is shown nibbling away at a Chinese cabbage leaf and is surrounded by grassy millet. Although he probably didn't have much singing ability, he has great personality!

Finished size: 14 x 14 inches; the design area measures 12 x 12 inches

Stitches: Stem and Straight

Materials: Black linen, 18 x 18 inches; three-strand Persian wool; #4 crewel needle; tracing paper; white dressmaker's carbon; artists' stretchers, 14 x 14 inches

Colors (numbers refer to Paternayan wool):

755 Dk. Blue, 1 full strand	534 Lt. Green, 4 full strands
765 Lt. Blue, 1 full strand	524 Dk. Green, 4 full strands
496 Off White, 3 full strands	454 Lt. Orange, 1 full strand
466 Tan, 4 full strands	434 Orange, 1 full strand
559 Med. Green, 4 full strands	260 Pink, 1 full strand
569 Med. Lt. Green, 1 full strand	164 Gray, 1 full strand
440 Gold, 4 full strands	050 Black, 1 full strand
492 Lt. Beige, 4 full strands	

Working instructions: (Color illustration page 76.)

- Enlarge the design and copy on tracing paper. Transfer the pattern to the fabric using dressmaker's carbon; do not transfer the *outline* of the design.

- Mount the fabric on the artists' stretchers.

- Separate the three-strand wool and use a *single* strand throughout. Consult the Color Chart for the placement of colors.

- With the exception of the accents in Straight stitch, the entire design is worked in Stem stitch, with approximately 10 stitches to the inch. Work the stitches in parallel rows, all in the same direction — not in alternating up and down or back and forth rows.

- Do the stems and leaves first; work from the bottom toward the top. Then do the cabbage. Work from the outline toward the center of the shape being filled. Do the veins on the cabbage in Straight stitch over the Stem stitch, using color 8 (Lt. Beige).

- Do the flower next. Work the centers first, then the outlines. Go on to the cricket. Work the legs, then the body, head, and antennae. Complete the corner leaves; work the centers, then the outlines.

PATTERN

enlarge to 12"

COLOR CHART

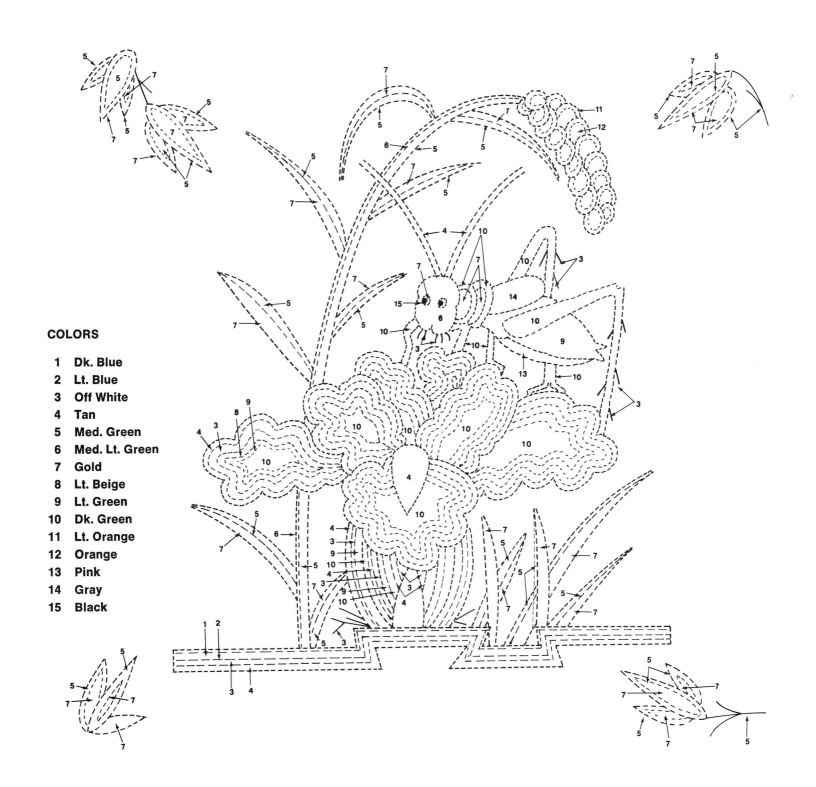

COLORS

1 Dk. Blue
2 Lt. Blue
3 Off White
4 Tan
5 Med. Green
6 Med. Lt. Green
7 Gold
8 Lt. Beige
9 Lt. Green
10 Dk. Green
11 Lt. Orange
12 Orange
13 Pink
14 Gray
15 Black

Fan holder. Petit point embroidery (Tent stitch) on silk gauze in colored silk floss. 12 ⅝ x 2 ⅜ inches. Chinese, Ch'ing dynasty, eighteenth–nineteenth century. Bequest of William Christian Paul, 1930. (Detail above; fan holder opposite.)

Chinese Mosaic

Fans have a long history in China, dating back to ancient times. Older Chinese fans were rigid and shaped something like a large lollipop. The more common folding fan was a Japanese invention, which was introduced into China via Korea in the eleventh century. Decorative cases for carrying the folding fans became fashionable costume accessories and were often given as presents. These were hung around the waist on a silk cord or carried in the sleeve.

Mosaic-type designs, like the pattern on this fan case, were common in Chinese decoration. This particular pattern is comprised of rosettes and auspicious symbols of joy and good fortune.

Finished size: Pattern of nine squares, 13 x 13 inches; each square, 4¼ x 4¼ inches

Stitches: Tent and Diagonal Tent (Basket Weave)

Materials: 13-mesh mono canvas, 17 x 17 inches; three-strand Persian wool; #20 tapestry needle; one-inch masking tape

Colors (amounts are for individual squares; numbers refer to Paternayan wool):

Design A	Design B
010 White, 4 full strands	010 White, 7 full strands
050 Black, 4 full strands	050 Black, 4 full strands
R74 Red, 1 full strand	642 Purple, 5 full strands
462 Brown, 4 full strands	R74 Red, 1 full strand
441 Yellow, 5 full strands	524 Dk. Green, 1 full strand
524 Green, 6 full strands	555 Lt. Green, 4 full strands
330 Med. Blue, 5 full strands	294 Pink, 4 full strands
395 Lt. Blue, 5 full strands	365 Dk. Blue, 2 full strands
	330 Med. Blue, 2 full strands
	395 Lt. Blue, 2 full strands

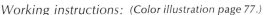

Working instructions: (*Color illustration page 77.*)

Use the designs individually for small objects like coasters, pin cushions, dolls' pillows, and doll house rugs, or combine the two designs in an alternating pattern for larger objects. The sample was designed to cover a 13-inch square pillow and contains nine squares. Each motif measures 59 x 59 mesh; this includes a Black border on all four sides. The sample of nine squares measures 175 x 175 mesh, since each motif shares a common Black outline with its neighbors.

- Bind the raw edges of the canvas with masking tape.

- Separate the three-strand wool and use *two* strands throughout.

- To work a design of nine alternating motifs, begin in the upper right corner of the canvas with Design A. To place the design on the canvas, mark a point two inches down from the top and two inches in from the right side. This intersection corresponds to the mesh in the upper right corner of Design A.

- Work the entire design in Tent stitch, or outline the shapes in Tent and fill in the larger areas in Diagonal Tent. The wool quantities given are sufficient for either method.

- Do the Black outlines first; work only one row of Black stitches between adjacent squares. Design A will then line up and flow into Design B.

- Outline the shapes in each motif, then fill in the center areas.

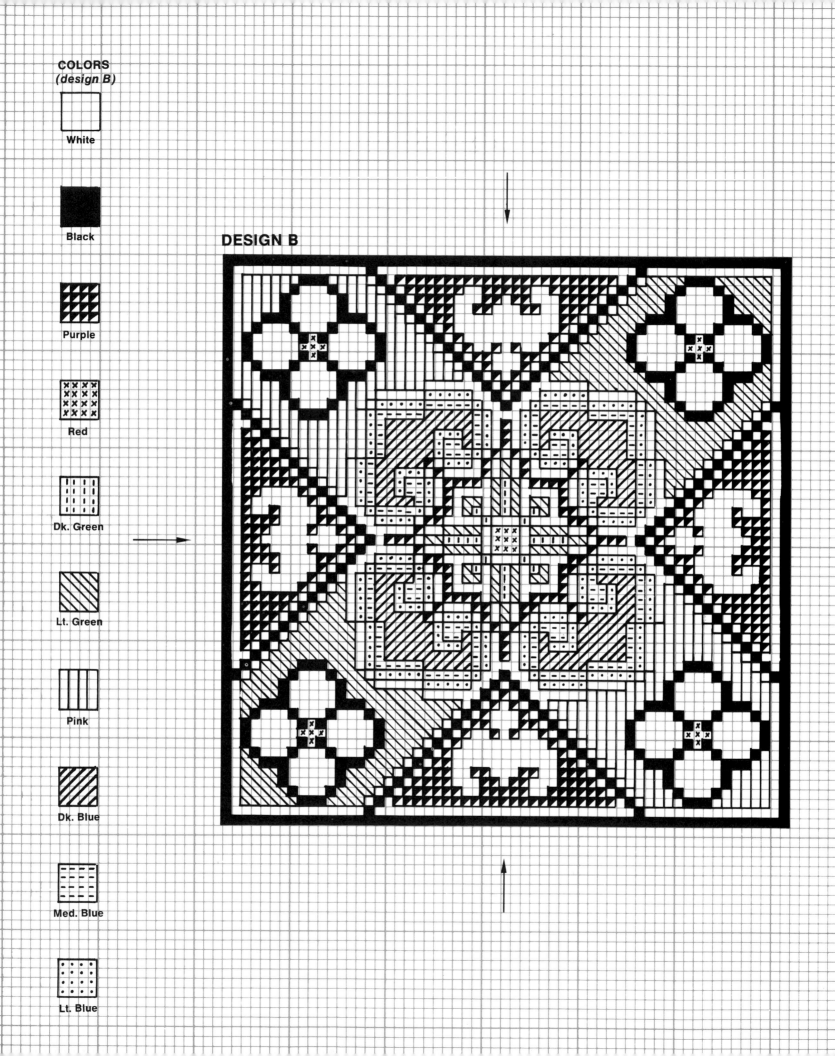

COLORS
(design B)

White

Black

Purple

Red

Dk. Green

Lt. Green

Pink

Dk. Blue

Med. Blue

Lt. Blue

DESIGN B

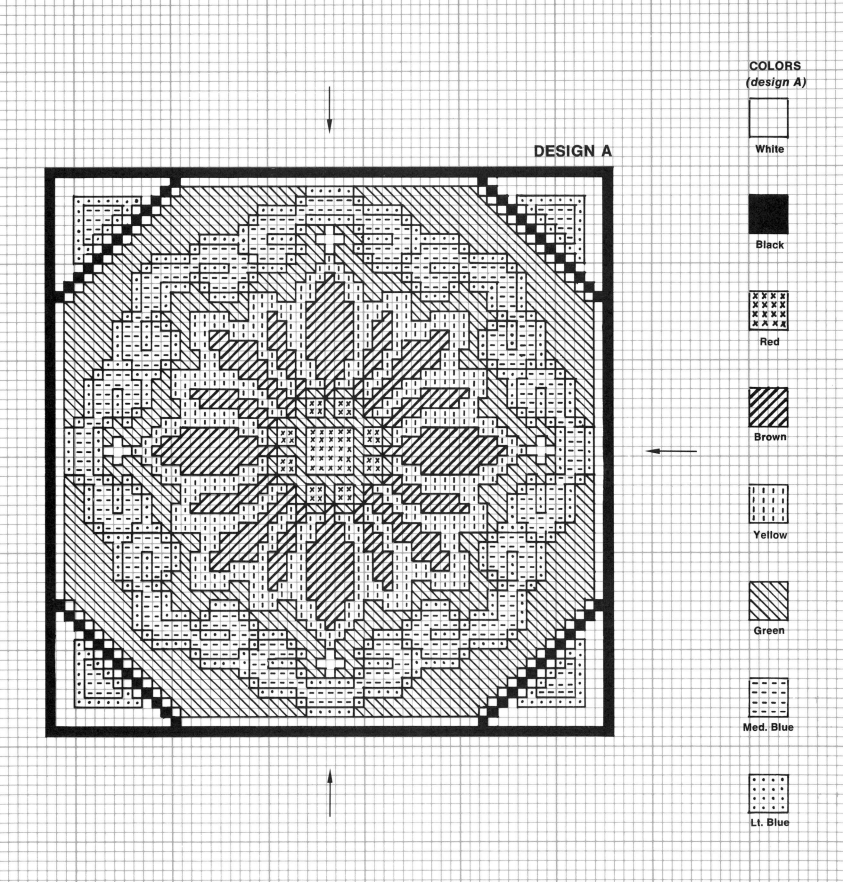

DESIGN A

COLORS
(design A)

White

Black

Red

Brown

Yellow

Green

Med. Blue

Lt. Blue

*Tambour-embroidered carpet by Zeruah Higley Guernsey (later Caswell),
worked in Chain stitch in colored wools on dyed homespun. 12 feet x
12 feet 6 inches. American (from Castleton, Vermont), dated 1835. Gift
of Katharine Keyes, in memory of her father, Homer Eaton Keyes, 1938.*

The Caswell carpet, as this rug has come to be called, is an outstanding example of American folk art of the nineteenth century. It was truly an ambitious project, for it took Zeruah Higley Guernsey the better part of five years to complete it. Like most ladies of her day she was accomplished in the "needle arts," and in the spirit of her colonial predecessors she sheared, carded, and spun the wools from her own sheep, dyed them, and wove the coarse homespun that was used as the foundation for the embroidery. Her father probably made the wooden needle she used to work the Chain stitch, for it is known that he was a manufacturer of spinning wheels and related tools.

The embroidery was done on a tambour (drum-shaped) frame; each of the sixty-six motifs was worked separately and the pieces later sewn together. The motifs include flowers, fruits, birds, puppies, kittens, and a charming scene of two young lovers. In the summer months a matching detachable hearth piece was added to the rug to help decorate a barren fireplace. The rug contains an interesting bit of local history, for two of the squares carry the initials of two Indians of the Potawatami tribe who were studying at the medical college in Castleton, Vermont. Each of the townspeople took turns boarding the students and it was undoubtedly during their stay at the Guernsey house that these two embroidery panels were worked.

Puppies

Finished size: 13 x 18 inches; the design measures 8¾ x 14 inches
Stitches: Chain and Split
Materials: Dark brown linen, 18 x 22 inches; three-strand Persian wool; #4 crewel needle; tracing paper; white dressmaker's carbon; artists' stretchers, 13 x 18 inches
Colors (numbers refer to Paternayan wool):

260 Lt. Pink, 6 full strands	145 Dk. Ochre, 6 full strands
255 Med. Pink, 6 full strands	386 Lt. Blue, 3 full strands
245 Dk. Pink, 5 full strands	330 Med. Blue, 3 full strands
020 Lt. Oatmeal, 25 full strands	334 Dk. Blue, 3 full strands
496 Lt. Yellow, 10 full strands	108 Charcoal Gray, 17 full strands
466 Lt. Ochre, 10 full strands	134 Tawny Gray, 8 full strands

Working instructions: (Color illustration page 78.)

- Enlarge the design photostatically. Copy the design on tracing paper and transfer to the linen, using white dressmaker's carbon. (If the outline is not strong enough, go over the lines with a white pencil.)

- Mount the fabric on artists' stretchers.

- Separate the three-strand wool and use a *single* strand throughout.

- The embroidery is done in two easy stitches: Chain and Split. Work the Chain stitches about 6 or 7 stitches to the inch and the Split stitches about 12 to the inch. Consult the Stitch and Color Chart for placement of the colors and the direction of the stitches.

- To begin, stitch the bodies of the puppies; start on the outline and work toward the center of the shape being filled. The arrows and dotted lines on the chart indicate only the direction of the stitches, not the number of rows to be worked; do as many rows as is necessary to fill in an area.

- Next, stitch the details of the eyes and paws.

- Do the background last. Stitch all the rows in the same direction; begin at the top and work toward the bottom.

- Complete by working the puppies' whiskers over the embroidered design.

Kittens

Finished size: 13 x 18 inches; the design measures 8¾ x 14 inches
Stitches: Chain and Split
Materials: Dark brown linen, 18 x 22 inches; three-strand Persian wool; #4 crewel needle; tracing paper; white dressmaker's carbon; artists' stretchers, 13 x 18 inches
Colors (numbers refer to Paternayan wool):

260 Lt. Pink, 6 full strands	466 Lt. Ochre, 7 full strands
255 Med. Pink, 4 full strands	145 Dk. Ochre, 5 full strands
245 Dk. Pink, 6 full strands	108 Charcoal Gray, 2 full strands
020 Lt. Oatmeal, 16 full strands	134 Tawny Gray, 20 full strands
496 Lt. Yellow, 7 full strands	

Working instructions: *(Color illustration page 79.)*
- Enlarge the design photostatically. Copy the design on tracing paper and transfer to the linen, using white dressmaker's carbon. (If the outline is not strong enough, go over the lines with a white pencil.)

- Mount the fabric on artists' stretchers.

- Separate the three-strand wool and use a *single* strand throughout.

- The embroidery is done in two easy stitches: Chain and Split. Work the Chain stitches about 6 or 7 to the inch and the Split stitches about 12 to the inch. Consult the Stitch and Color Chart for placement of the colors and the direction of the stitches.

- To begin, stitch the bodies of the kittens; start on the outline and work toward the center of the shape being filled. The arrows and dotted lines on the chart indicate only the direction of the stitches, not the number of rows to be worked; do as many rows as is necessary to fill in an area.

- Next, stitch the details of the eyes and paws.

- Do the background last. Stitch all the rows in the same direction; begin at the top and work toward the bottom.

- Complete by working the kittens' whiskers over the embroidered design.

Detail from the Caswell carpet showing the puppies and kittens that inspired the adaptations.

PATTERN

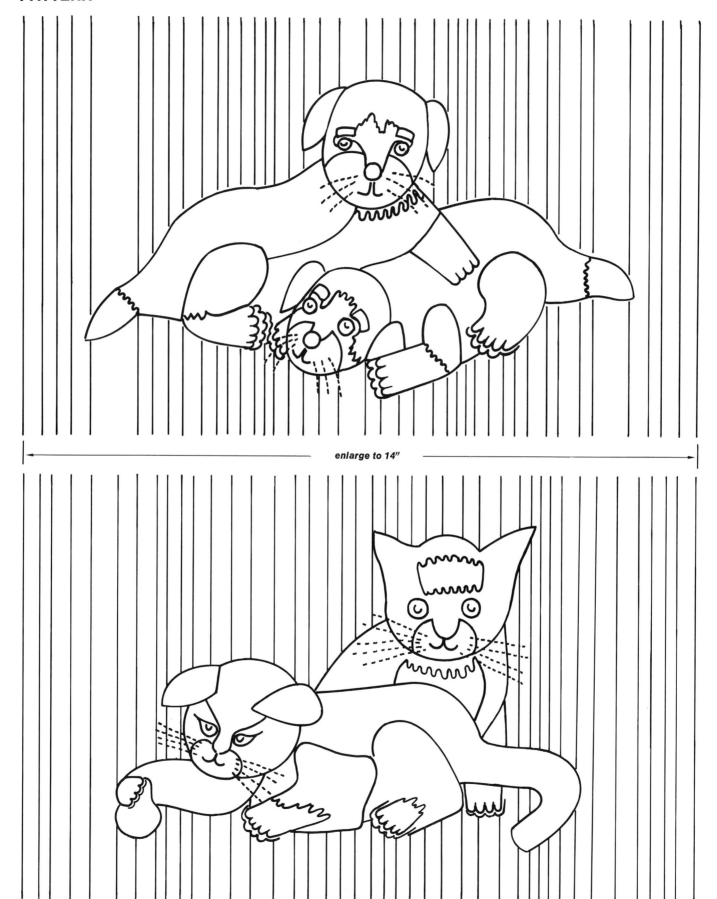

enlarge to 14"

STITCH AND COLOR CHART

COLORS

1	Lt. Pink	9	Med. Blue
2	Med. Pink	10	Dk. Blue
3	Dk. Pink	11	Charcoal Gray
4	Lt. Oatmeal	12	Tawny Gray
5	Lt. Yellow		
6	Lt. Ochre	**STITCHES**	
7	Dk. Ochre		
8	Lt. Blue	Chain	– – – –
		Split	ᴑᴑᴑᴑᴑᴑ

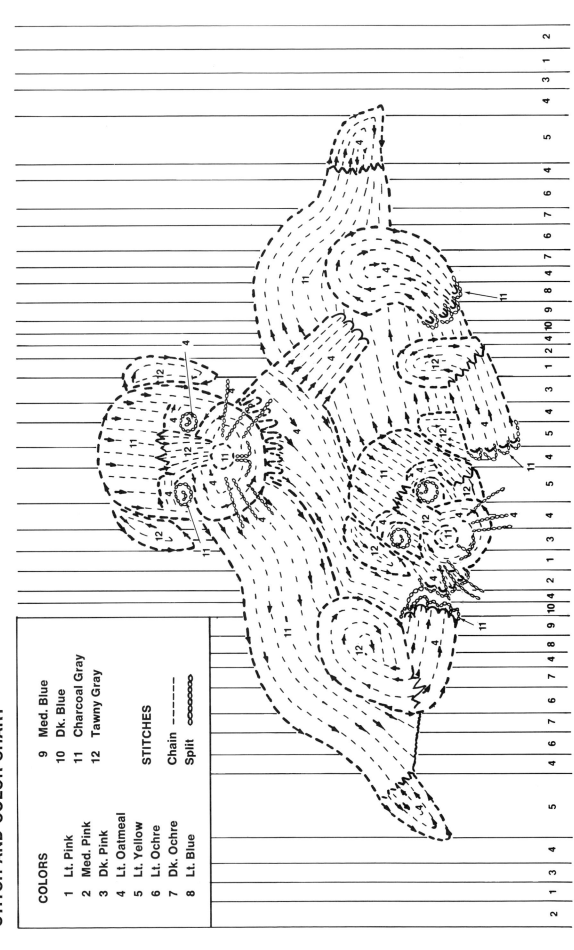

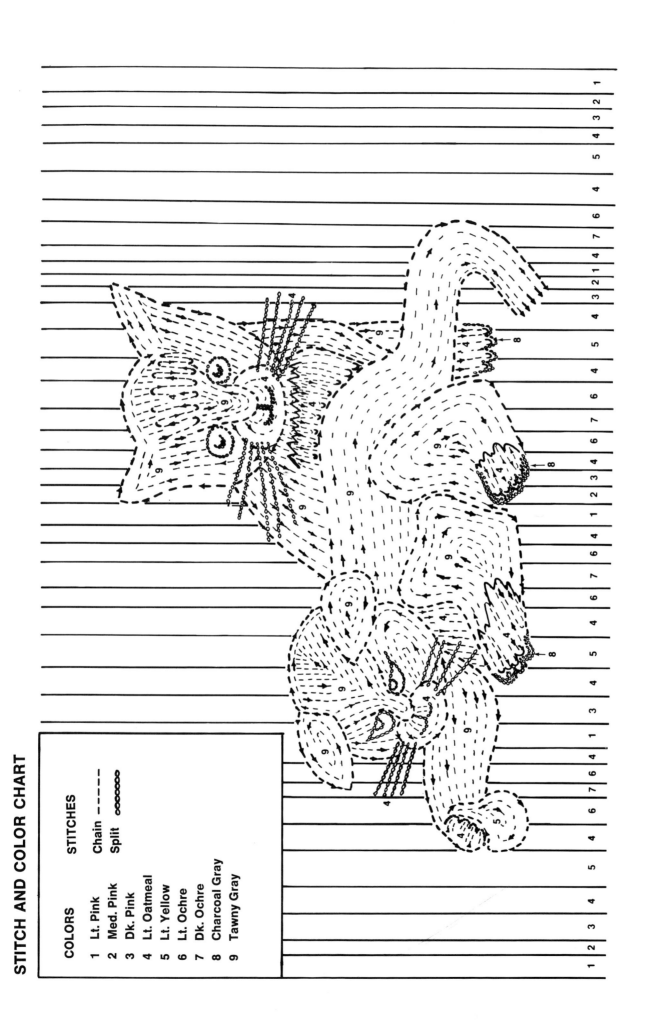

STITCH AND COLOR CHART

COLORS

STITCHES

Chain – – –
Split ○○○○○○

1 Lt. Pink
2 Med. Pink
3 Dk. Pink
4 Lt. Oatmeal
5 Lt. Yellow
6 Lt. Ochre
7 Dk. Ochre
8 Charcoal Gray
9 Tawny Gray

*Fragment of a peasant costume. Linen embroidery in silk thread, worked
in upright stitches. 4¾ x 3¾ inches. Albanian or Montenegrin,
eighteenth–nineteenth century. Rogers Fund, 1909.*

Earth-Colored Peasant Repeat

Traditionally the peasant's dress differed from that of his "betters" because his garments had to withstand hard wear. Very often the dyes available were limited, mostly to simple earth colors. Since the designs on the old costumes were copied and recopied in later centuries, the earth colors continued to appear with some frequency even after a wide variety of dyes became available.

Many peasant embroideries were done in long stitches that could be worked quickly and in a coarse manner. Some authorities believe that Florentine stitch may have originated from peasant embroideries of this type.

Finished size: 14 x 14 inches

Stitch: Florentine

Materials: 13-mesh mono canvas, 18 x 18 inches; three-strand Persian wool; #20
   tapestry needle; one-inch masking tape; 4H pencil

Colors (numbers refer to Paternayan wool):

114 Brown, 25 full strands	531 Gold, 35 full strands
136 Beige, 95 full strands	010 White, 35 full strands

Working instructions: *(Color illustration page 80.)*

Since this is a repeat design, the overall size of the finished embroidery is
determined by the object to be covered. The sample was designed to cover a
14-inch square pillow, but the pattern would be striking on a handbag or as a
chair covering.

- Before cutting the canvas, be sure to measure carefully the object to be
  covered; allow additional canvas for any finishing necessary, and add to that
  at least two inches on all sides for blocking. The sample measures H. 174 x
  W. 191 mesh; the 18-inch square canvas allows two inches on all sides for
  blocking.

- Bind the raw edges of the canvas with masking tape. Locate the center of the
  canvas by folding it in half, then in quarters. Mark the center lines, using a
  4H pencil.

- Separate the three-strand wool and use *two* strands throughout.

- Turn the graph on its side and work the pattern in Florentine stitch, covering
  two horizontal threads of the canvas; where a one-box stitch is indicated,
  cover only *one* horizontal thread; where a three-box stitch is indicated (this
  appears only in the background), cover *three* horizontal threads.

- Begin with the central motif. Do the framework in Gold first; then do the
  Beige, carefully noting the one-box stitches in this row. Go on to the Dk.
  Brown. Continue to work from the outline toward the center of each shape.

- After the framework is complete, fill in the checkerboard. Work the White
  stitches first, then fill in the Beige. Do the Beige background last.

- In completing the pattern, end the design with the checkerboard rather than
  in the middle of a repeat (see the color illustration).

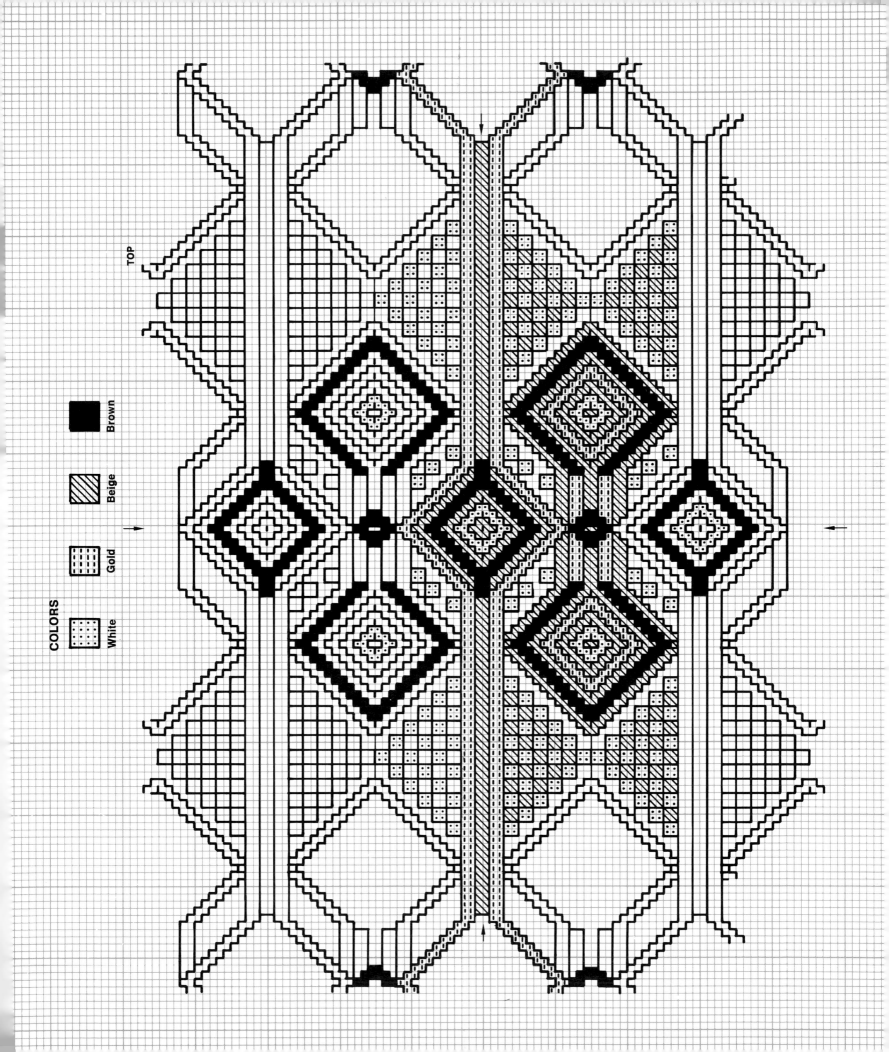

COLORS

■ Brown

▨ Beige

▦ Gold

⊡ White

TOP

Envelope purse in petit point embroidery (Tent stitch), worked in colored wools on canvas. The bag is lined with calendered (polished) wool, or tammy cloth, and has a metal closure. 7 ⅛ x 4 inches. American, about 1760. Rogers Fund, 1942.

Pockets and purses were popular accessories in eighteenth-century America. Purses were usually fashioned for men and elegant examples were displayed with pride at social gatherings and on special occasions. Women commonly tied pockets around their waists, concealed under their skirts; they reached them through slits in their skirts and petticoats.

Most of these accessories, for both men and women, were embroidered with floral motifs, and this envelope purse (probably for a man) is typical of the period in this respect. Its patterns include flowers and fruits commonly found in all types of colonial embroidery — chrysanthemums, carnations, pinks, wild strawberries.

Adaptation mounted as an envelope purse.

Flower Garden with Wild Strawberries

Finished size: 17 x 12 inches, flat; 6 x 12 inches, folded

Stitches: Tent and Diagonal Tent (Basket Weave)

Materials: 13-mesh mono canvas, 22 x 16 inches; three-strand Persian wool; #20 tapestry needle; one-inch masking tape

Colors (numbers refer to Paternayan wool):

011 White, 30 full strands	893 Lavender, 28 full strands
265 Pink, 15 full strands	891 Purple, 15 full strands
R86 Coral, 20 full strands	531 Gold, 48 full strands
R69 Red, 15 full strands	512 Green, 80 full strands
467 Yellow, 15 full strands	314 Blue, 40 full strands

Working instructions: *(Color illustration page 115.)*

The design measures H. 225 x W. 162 mesh. The 22 x 16–inch size canvas allows at least two inches all around for blocking.

- Bind the raw edges of the canvas with masking tape.

- Separate the three-strand wool and use *two* strands throughout.

- The entire design may be stitched in Tent, or outline the shapes in Tent and fill in the larger areas in Diagonal Tent. The wool quantities given are sufficient for either method; however, if the design is worked in the purse shape, I recommend using Diagonal Tent wherever possible so that blocking will be easier.

- Begin the pattern in the upper right corner. Mark a point on the canvas two inches down from the top and two inches in from the right side; this intersection corresponds to the corner mesh of the design (if worked as a complete rectangle) and the square in the upper right corner on the chart (again, if worked as a complete rectangle). If you plan to work the pattern as a rectangle (for a pillow or bench cover), begin at this point. For the purse shape, the starting stitch is 20 mesh directly below the corner mesh.

- The easiest way to work the pattern is to outline the shapes first, then fill in the centers. Do the background areas last.

COLORS

White

Pink

Coral

Red

Yellow

Lavender

Purple

Gold

Green

Blue

104

Altar frontal. Embroidery on double-mesh canvas in colored silk threads, worked in Cross, Satin, Stem, and Florentine stitches. 41 x 62 inches. Italian, seventeenth–eighteenth century. Gift of Susan Dwight Bliss, 1955. (Detail opposite.)

Roses and Carnations

The Catholic Church was historically one of the greatest patrons of embroidery, although the output of the Middle Ages was never equaled in later centuries. By the seventeenth and eighteenth centuries, ecclesiastical embroidery had become highly decorative, the themes more secular, and the designs for the most part were heavily reliant upon motifs from the Renaissance.

In this altar frontal the symbols of the Eucharist are confined to the central medallion, the rest of the embroidery being covered with a beautiful repeating pattern of roses and carnations. The border decoration contains flower sprays and large potted flowers between flanking stags.

For the adaptation I used the allover repeat floral pattern, carefully "counted" from the Museum's original.

Finished size: 21 x 16⅝ inches

Stitches: Cross and Florentine

Materials: 11-mesh tan-colored penelope canvas; six-strand mercerized cotton; #20 tapestry needle; one-inch masking tape; 4H pencil

Colors (numbers refer to D.M.C. cotton):

310 Black	223 Dk. Rose
712 White	758 Apricot
828 Lt. Blue	471 Green
813 Dk. Blue	726 Yellow

Working instructions: *(Color illustration page 116.)*

Since this is a repeat design the overall size of the finished embroidery is determined by the object to be covered. The sample was designed to cover a footstool, but the pattern is suitable for many other objects.

- Normally penelope canvas is worked with the selvage on either the right or left side; for this pattern, work the embroidery with the selvage either on the top or bottom. Be sure to purchase canvas *wide* enough to position the pattern correctly on the object you are covering.

- Before cutting the canvas, measure the object again, carefully; allow additional canvas for any finishing necessary and add to that at least an inch on all sides for blocking.

- Bind off the raw edges of the canvas with masking tape. Locate the center of the canvas by folding it in half, then in quarters. Mark the center lines on double horizontal and double vertical threads, using a 4H pencil.

- Work the pattern and the background using all six strands (full strength) of the D.M.C. cotton throughout.

- To work the design, begin in the center of the canvas with the central motif. Do the Black outline first, using Cross stitches worked individually from left to right (see instructions for Cross stitch). Be sure that all the stitches slant in the same direction; in this case the final half crosses should slant from lower left to upper right. When working the stitches in the opposite direction, turn the canvas and the charted graph on their sides and proceed from right to left, with the final half crosses slanting from lower right to upper left. As a helpful reminder, put a little marker in the corner of the canvas to indicate the direction of the final half crosses.

- After completing the Black outline, fill in the interior of the flower; work each color as if it were an outline and follow the contour of the rose shape. Again, work Cross stitches individually. Complete the Dk. Blue outline around the rose and go on to the next shape.

- Always begin with the Black outline, then fill in the center colors. The Cross stitches will look neater if they are worked as individual stitches; however, the Green stems on the carnations may be filled in using the two-journey method of half crosses. The background is filled in after the design is complete. Florentine stitch is used as a lovely contrast to the Cross-stitch design. It is worked here in an unusual manner that produces small openings on the surface of the embroidery with a single canvas thread peeking through. The Museum's original was worked in the same way. Here the stitch is worked over two mesh on the canvas in groups of two stitches. (Remember on penelope a mesh is the intersection of double vertical and double horizontal threads.)

- Begin the first Florentine stitch by bringing the needle out *between* a double vertical thread, enlarging the space slightly; go in two mesh directly above, again between a double vertical thread. The second upright stitch is worked in the regular canvas spaces, without splitting. Continue as for Florentine stitch worked in horizontal rows (see stitch instructions for Florentine), always splitting the vertical canvas threads for the first stitch in each group of two stitches.

- Work all the rows of Florentine from left to right by turning the canvas upside down after each row.

- When only one mesh appears where the Florentine stitches meet the Cross stitches, work either upright stitches over one mesh or fill in with a Cross stitch using the Yellow background color.

SELVAGE

SELVAGE

COLORS

■	⬚	⫼	⊠	▨	⬚	▨	☐
Black	White	Lt. Blue	Dk. Blue	Dk. Rose	Apricot	Green	Yellow

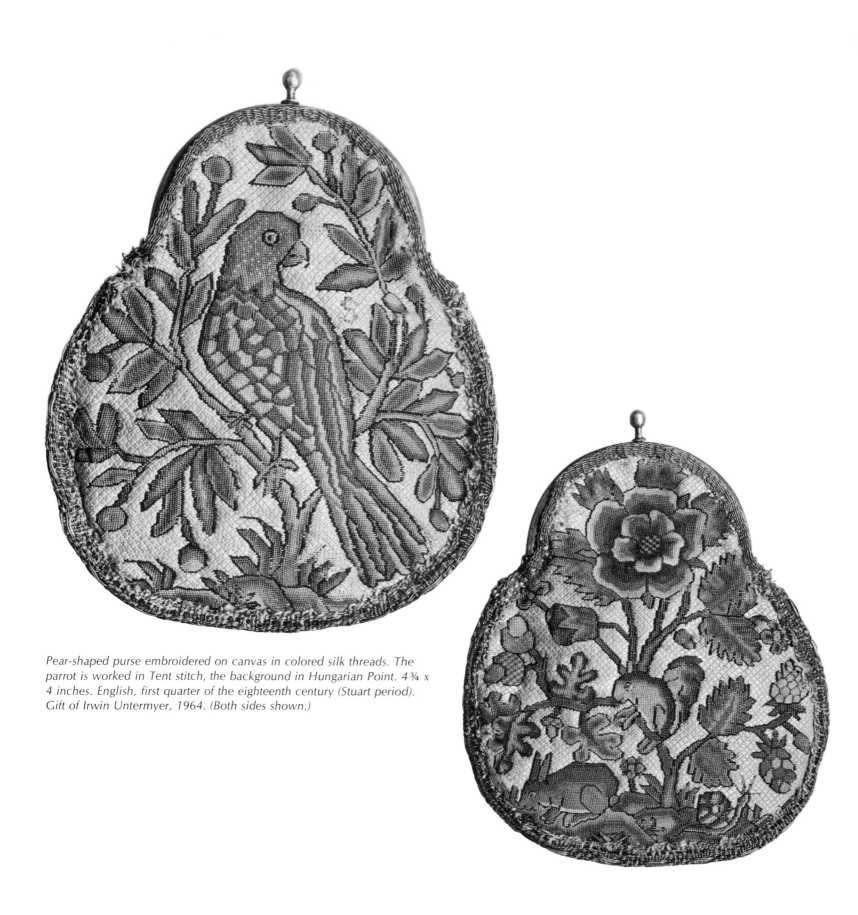

Pear-shaped purse embroidered on canvas in colored silk threads. The parrot is worked in Tent stitch, the background in Hungarian Point. 4 ¾ x 4 inches. English, first quarter of the eighteenth century (Stuart period). Gift of Irwin Untermyer, 1964. (Both sides shown.)

This dainty pear-shaped purse was probably reserved for special occasions and may have carried a charm, a tiny prayer book, or sweet herbs and spices.

The embroidery of personal and household articles became popular in England in the early sixteenth century, about the time of the Reformation. Almost every Englishwoman was trained in needlework, regardless of her station in life. Beautiful silk and metal threads were available for embroidery, and by the mid-sixteenth century fine steel needles were being manufactured in England. For inspiration the embroiderer had only to look into her garden or consult contemporary herbals, bestiaries, or books of emblems. In the sixteenth and seventeenth centuries pattern books for embroidery were available and were commonly used.

Parrot in a Pear-Shaped Tree

Finished size: 14 x 14 inches

Stitches: Tent and Mosaic

Materials: 13-mesh mono canvas, 18 x 18 inches; three-strand Persian wool; #20 tapestry needle; one-inch masking tape; 4H pencil

Colors (numbers refer to Paternayan wool):

020 Off White, 150 full strands	386 Lt. Blue, 5 full strands
441 Yellow, 6 full strands	330 Dk. Blue, 5 full strands
550 Lt. Green, 20 full strands	232 Dk. Rose, 18 full strands
288 Lt. Rose, 5 full strands	145 Dk. Brown, 8 full strands
466 Lt. Brown, 9 full strands	510 Dk. Green, 25 full strands

Working instructions: (Color illustration page 113.)

The central motif measures H. 145 x W. 122 mesh. Since the design is based on this central motif, the amount of background area is determined by the overall size of the object to be covered. The sample was designed to cover a 14-inch square pillow, and the 18-inch square canvas will accommodate the embroidery plus two inches on all sides for blocking. The design would also be lovely on a handbag, a chair seat, or a round footstool. If you are planning to use it in this way, be sure to measure the object carefully before cutting the canvas; allow additional canvas for any finishing necessary, and add to that at least two inches on all sides for blocking.

- Bind the raw edges of the canvas with masking tape. Locate the center of the canvas by folding it in half, then in quarters. Mark the center lines with a 4H pencil.

- Separate the three-strand wool and use *two* strands throughout.

- Using Tent stitch, begin with the bird; then do the leaves and tree. It is easiest to outline the shapes first, then fill in the centers.

- Do the background last, using Mosaic stitch. This stitch may be worked in vertical rows (from top to bottom), or in horizontal rows (from right to left). To achieve an even texture on the face of the embroidery, maintain one direction throughout. Begin the background in the upper right corner.

COLORS

Off White Yellow Lt. Green Lt. Rose Lt. Brown Lt. Blue Dk. Blue Dk. Rose Dk. Brown Dk. Green

PARROT IN A PEAR-SHAPED TREE   *From a pear-shaped purse, English, first quarter of the eighteenth century.*

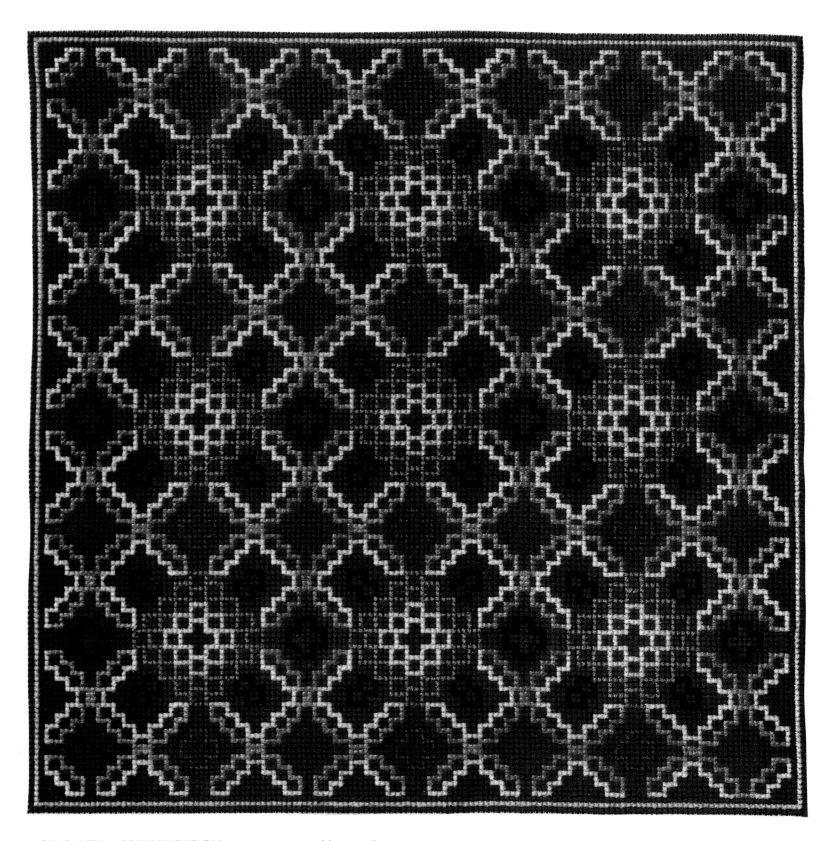

PEASANT HAPPINESS DESIGN   *From a peasant blouse, Albanian or Montenegrin, eighteenth–nineteenth century.*

114

FLOWER GARDEN WITH WILD STRAWBERRIES   *From a petit point purse, American, about 1760.*   115

PERUVIAN PUMA GOD   *From a tapestry-woven costume, Peruvian, Tiahuanaco II Culture, about A.D. 700–800.*

Opposite page: ROSES AND CARNATIONS   *From an embroidered altar frontal, Italian, seventeenth–eighteenth century.*

118

FLOWERS OF THE FOUR SEASONS — 1   *From an embroidered sleeveband, Chinese, nineteenth century.*

FLOWERS OF THE FOUR SEASONS — 2   *From an embroidered sleeveband, Chinese, nineteenth century.*

TURKISH PEACOCK   *From an embroidered bedspread, Albanian (Janina), eighteenth century.*

Peasant Happiness Design

By 1800 decorative peasant costumes or "folk dress" had evolved for use on special occasions — church festivals, weddings, and christenings. Many of these were beautifully embroidered with geometric-type Cross stitch patterns that were handed down from generation to generation.

This pattern, a cross surrounded by concentric circles, is frequently found on costumes as well as on ceremonial articles such as church shawls and christening cloths. The cross was one of the earliest tokens used to ward off the "evil eye," and it was used traditionally to convey wishes for happiness and well-being — especially to newborn infants.

Fragment of a peasant blouse (top right). Cross stitch embroidery on canvas in colored wools. 4⅜ x 3⅞ inches. Albanian or Montenegrin, eighteenth–nineteenth century. Rogers Fund, 1909.

Finished size: 14 x 14 inches

Stitch: Cross

Materials: 11-mesh white penelope canvas, 18 x 18 inches; three-strand Persian
  wool; #20 tapestry needle; one-inch masking tape; 4H pencil

Colors (numbers refer to Paternayan wool):

010 White, 26 full strands	350 Blue, 8 full strands
437 Yellow, 12 full strands	108 Charcoal, 15 full strands
555 Green, 15 full strands	810 Red, 120 full strands
860 Pink, 28 full strands	

Working instructions: *(Color illustration page 114.)*

The sample measures 150 x 150 mesh. Since this is a repeat design, the overall
size of the finished embroidery is determined by the object to be covered. The
sample was designed to cover a 14-inch square pillow, and the 18-inch square
canvas will accommodate for the pillow plus two inches on all sides for blocking.
The pattern might also be used for a handbag, to cover a chair or even a book. If
you are planning to use it in this way, be sure to measure carefully the object to
be covered before cutting the canvas; allow additional canvas for any finishing
necessary and add to that at least two inches on all sides for blocking.

- Bind the raw edges of the canvas with masking tape. Locate the center of the
  canvas by folding it in half, then in quarters. Mark the center lines on double
  horizontal and double vertical threads, using a 4H pencil.

- Separate the three-strand wool and use a *single* strand throughout.

- Begin the design in the center of the canvas. Work the cross in White first,
  then the Yellow circle, then the Green, White, Pink, etc. Fill in the Red
  background last.

- Border the design with a row of Red, then a row of Yellow, then one or two
  more rows of Red. (See color illustration.)

COLORS

White   Yellow   Green   Pink   Blue   Charcoal   Red

SELVAGE

Fragment, possibly part of a shirt or mantle. Tapestry woven in colored wools. 12¾ x 19¾ inches. Peruvian (Highland Region), about A.D. 700–800 (Tiahuanaco II Culture). Gift of George D. Pratt, 1932. (Detail above; fragment opposite.)

Some of the finest woven textiles ever made come from this pre-Inca Andean civilization. The surviving pieces are mostly fragments of wearing apparel, richly decorated with religious and mythological symbols. This design, perhaps from a shirt or mantle, shows figures with human heads and arms, and puma tails. The ancient Peruvians practiced both sun and moon worship and representations of pumas were very common, as the cat was considered the "Mother of the Moon." The curious glyphlike forms in the border are a kind of shorthand indicating animal parts or animal markings; the diamond shape possibly represents an eye and the zigzag W shape possibly the tail.

124

Peruvian Puma God

Finished size: 14¼ x 15⅜ inches

Stitches: Tent and Diagonal Tent (Basket Weave)

Materials: 13-mesh mono canvas, 19 x 20 inches; three-strand Persian wool; #20 tapestry needle; one-inch masking tape

Colors (numbers refer to Paternayan wool):

015 Off White, 58 full strands	433 Gold, 25 full strands
453 Lt. Yellow, 50 full strands	231 Red, 40 full strands
322 Lt. Blue, 20 full strands	201 Brown, 40 full strands
281 Pink, 20 full strands	

Working instructions: *(Color illustration page 117.)*

The design measures H. 190 x W. 200 mesh. The 19 x 20–inch canvas allows about two extra inches all around for blocking.

- Bind the raw edges of the canvas with masking tape.

- Separate the three-strand wool and use *two* strands throughout.

- The entire design may be stitched in regular Tent, or outline the shapes in Tent and fill in the larger areas in Diagonal Tent. The wool quantities given are sufficient for either method.

- Begin the pattern in the upper right corner. To place the design on the canvas, measure two inches down from the top, and two inches in from the right side. The mesh at this point corresponds to the corner mesh of the design and the square in the upper right corner of the chart. Follow the chart for the design and placement of colors. An easy method of working is to outline the shapes first, then fill in the center areas.

COLORS

Off White	Lt. Yellow	Lt. Blue	Pink	Gold	Red	Brown

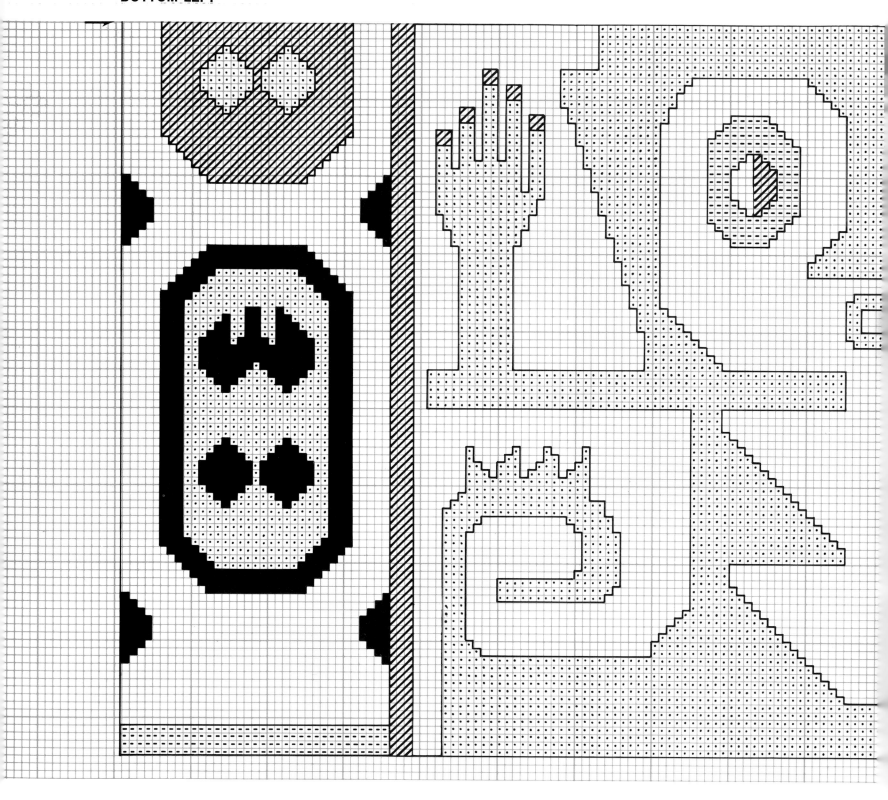

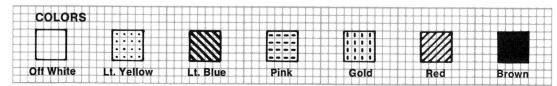

128

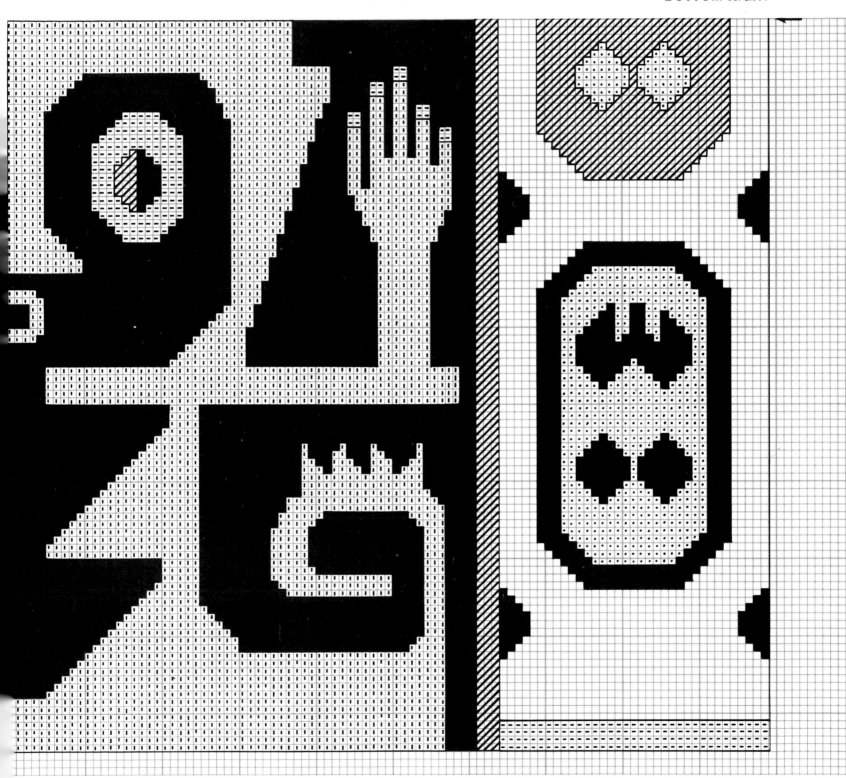

Flowers of the Four Seasons-I

The narrow bands that decorate the sleeves of Chinese costumes are often stunning examples of Chinese embroidery. The sleevebands shown here are worked almost entirely in Satin stitch — a stitch known to the Chinese since ancient times. Satin stitch was extremely well suited to the fine silk threads produced in the Orient, as the long, smooth stitches emphasized the sheen of the silk.

The designs found on sleevebands can sometimes be traced to specific episodes in Chinese novels or poetry, or very often they are of lovely garden scenes and landscapes. The two bands that inspired these adaptations are embroidered with garden scenes which contain flowers of the four seasons. The roses in the first scene are symbols for summer. In the second, the chrysanthemums symbolize fall; the narcissus, spring; and the *nanten,* a flowering shrub which produces red berries, symbolizes fortitude in winter (the *nanten* was also a symbol for the "good wife"). Both scenes contain elements typical of the Chinese garden — the decorative rocks, flowing water, and simple footbridges.

Finished size: The design measures 18¾ x 12 inches

Stitches: Satin, Stem, Straight, Chain, Long-and-Short, Couching

Materials: Gray-blue linen, 24 x 18 inches; six-strand and pearl (twisted) cotton; #18 chenille needle; tracing paper; blue dressmaker's carbon; artists' stretchers, 22 x 16 inches

Colors (numbers refer to D.M.C. cotton):

All colors pertain to the six-strand mercerized thread unless pearl is indicated.

352 Apricot, 1 skein	712 White, 1 skein
945 Lt. Apricot, 1 skein	(six-strand), 1 skein (pearl)
503 Cool Green, 2 skeins	369 Lt. Mint Green, 1 skein
500 Dk. Green, 1 skein	744 Yellow, 1 skein (pearl)
471 Yellow/Green, 2 skeins	760 Copper, 1 skein
320 Med. Green, 2 skeins	612 Lt. Brown, 1 skein
311 Dk. Blue, 1 skein	844 Charcoal Brown, 1 skein
3325 Lt. Blue, 1 skein	

Working instructions: (Color illustration page 118.)

- Enlarge the design photostatically. Trace the design and transfer it to the linen, using dressmaker's carbon. Mount the fabric on artists' stretchers.

- Separate the six-strand cotton and use *three* strands throughout. Use *one* strand (full strength) of the pearl cotton for the bridge (Yellow and White) and *two* strands of the White pearl cotton for the couched border.

- Consult the Stitch and Color Chart for placement of colors, stitches, and direction of stitches.

- There is no particular order recommended for working the embroidery, though skipping around from area to area is suggested for variety.

Sleeveband, one of a pair, from a woman's informal robe. Embroidered on blue satin in twisted silk threads. 41½ x 3¾ inches. Chinese, nineteenth century. Bequest of William Christian Paul, 1930. (Detail opposite.)

Flowers of the Four Seasons-2

Finished size: The design measures 18¾ x 12 inches

Stitches: Satin, Stem, Straight, Chain, Long-and-Short, French Knot, and Couching

Materials: Gray-blue linen, 24 x 18 inches; six-strand and pearl (twisted) cotton; #18 chenille needle; tracing paper; blue dressmaker's carbon; artists' stretchers, 22 x 16 inches

Colors (numbers refer to D.M.C. cotton):

All colors pertain to the six-strand mercerized thread unless pearl is indicated.

369 Lt. Mint Green, 2 skeins	352 Apricot, 1 skein
471 Yellow/Green, 2 skeins	760 Copper, 1 skein
320 Med. Green, 2 skeins	945 Lt. Apricot, 1 skein
504 Lt. Cool Green, 1 skein	3325 Lt. Blue, 1 skein
503 Cool Green, 2 skeins	(six-strand), 1 skein (pearl)
500 Dk. Green, 1 skein	311 Dk. Blue, 1 skein
744 Yellow, 1 skein (pearl)	712 White, 1 skein (six-strand), 1 skein
745 Lt. Yellow, 1 skein	(pearl)
	844 Charcoal Brown, 1 skein

Working instructions: *(Color illustration page 119.)*

- Enlarge the design photostatically. Trace the design and transfer it to the linen, using dressmaker's carbon.

- Mount the fabric on the artists' stretchers.

- Separate the six-strand cotton and use *three* strands throughout, except when working French Knots; for these, use *all* six strands. Use *one* strand (full strength) of the pearl cotton on the bridge (Yellow and Lt. Blue) and *two* strands of the White pearl cotton for the couched border.

- Consult the Stitch and Color Chart for placement of colors, stitches, and direction of stitches.

- There is no particular order recommended for working the embroidery, though skipping around from area to area is suggested for variety.

Sleeveband, one of a pair, from a woman's informal robe. Embroidered on blue satin in twisted silk threads. 41½ x 3¾ inches. Chinese, nineteenth century. Bequest of William Christian Paul, 1930. (Detail opposite.)

enlarge to 12"

STITCH AND COLOR CHART

COLORS

1 Apricot
2 Lt. Apricot
3 Cool Green
4 Dk. Green
5 Yellow/Green
6 Med. Green
7 Dk. Blue
8 Lt. Blue
9 White
10 Lt. Mint Green
11 Yellow
12 Copper
13 Lt. Brown
14 Charcoal Brown

STITCHES

Satin
Stem
Straight
Chain
Long-and-Short   A
Couching   B

135

enlarge to 12"

STITCH AND COLOR CHART

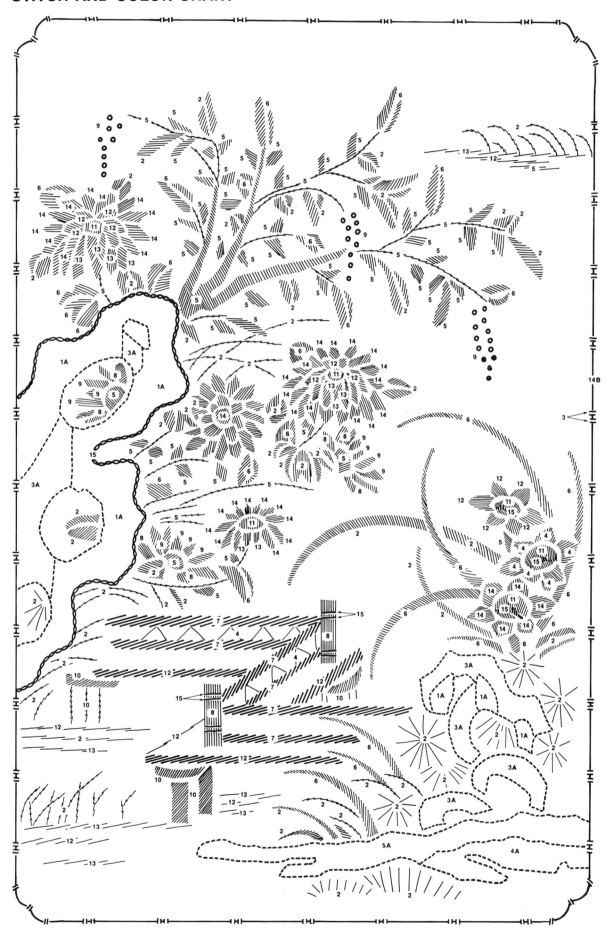

COLORS

1 Lt. Mint Green
2 Yellow/Green
3 Med. Green
4 Lt. Cool Green
5 Cool Green
6 Dk. Green
7 Yellow
8 Lt. Yellow
9 Apricot
10 Copper
11 Lt. Apricot
12 Lt. Blue
13 Dk. Blue
14 White
15 Charcoal Brown

STITCHES

Satin
Stem
Straight
Chain
Long-and-Short A
French Knot
Couching B

137

Fragment. Linen embroidery in colored silk threads, worked predominately in Herringbone stitch. 20½ x 53 inches. Ottoman Turkish, Albanian (Janina), eighteenth century. Bequest of Richard B. Seager, 1926. (Detail opposite.)

Turkish Peacock

Janina, seat of a notorious Turkish pasha in the late eighteenth century, was known for its embroideries. The surviving peasant embroideries from the area are mostly fragments from large bedspreads; apparently the central portions of these spreads were plain undecorated linen, and to make a more saleable piece, the embroidered borders were removed and pieced together. If you look carefully at the illustration of this embroidery, you can see the horizontal seam across the middle where the borders were sewn together.

Janina borders were embroidered almost entirely in Herringbone stitch and were decorated with floral motifs. The one in the Metropolitan's collection is unusual in that the design incorporates flowers with birds — peacocks, sprays of roses, tulips, and pomegranates.

Finished size: The design measures 10½ x 13 inches

Stitches: Closed Herringbone, Back, Straight, and Satin

Materials: Natural-colored linen, 20 x 24 inches; six-strand mercerized cotton; #18 chenille needle; tracing paper; blue dressmaker's carbon; artists' stretchers, 16 x 20 inches

Colors (numbers refer to D.M.C. cotton):

347 Red, 3 skeins	3688 Pink, 2 skeins
825 Blue, 2 skeins	739 Beige, 2 skeins
367 Green, 2 skeins	712 White, 2 skeins
839 Brown, 4 skeins	

Working instructions: *(Color illustration page 120.)*

- Enlarge the design photostatically. Copy the design on tracing paper and transfer to the linen, using dressmaker's carbon.

- Mount the fabric on the artists' stretchers.

- When working Closed Herringbone, Straight, and Satin stitches, use the six-strand cotton full strength throughout. For the outlines in Back stitch, separate the six strands and use only *four* of them.

- Consult the Stitch and Color Chart for placement of colors and stitches.

- Do all Straight and Back stitch outlines using color 4 (Brown).

- Begin the embroidery wherever you like, but always outline the shapes in Back stitch *after* they have been filled in with Herringbone stitch.

enlarge to 13"

140

STITCH AND COLOR CHART

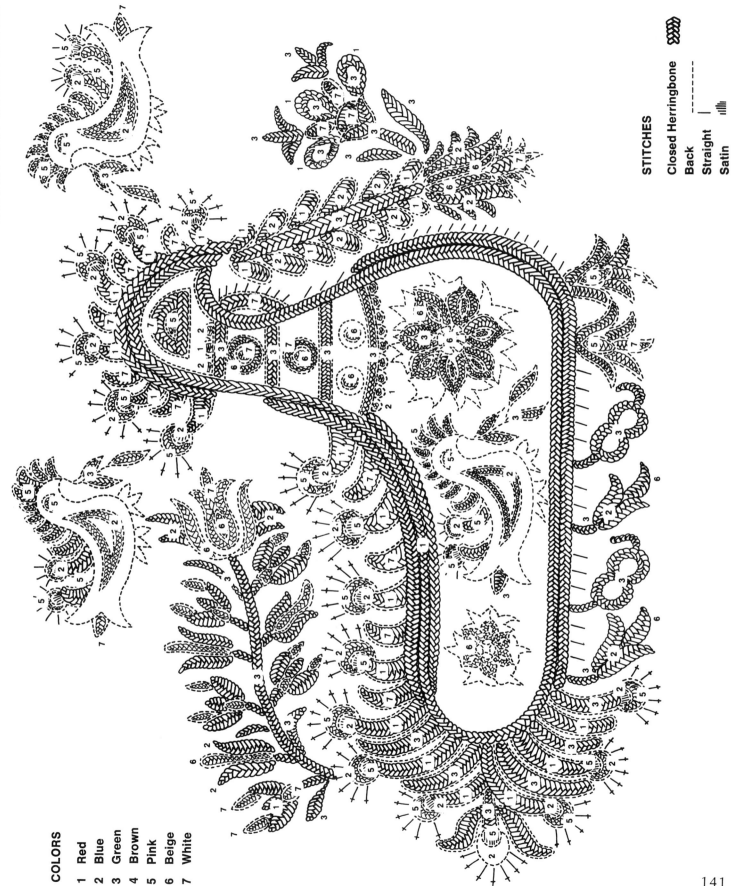

COLORS
1 Red
2 Blue
3 Green
4 Brown
5 Pink
6 Beige
7 White

STITCHES

Closed Herringbone

Back

Straight

Satin

A Gallery of Stitches

About ten years ago a prominent needlework author wrote, "The Metropolitan in New York is the best source for seeing how the old stitches were once used." She was referring to the Museum's Textile Study Room, which houses one of the finest collections of embroideries and woven fabrics in the country. Unfortunately, many people can't come to New York frequently or don't have the necessary hours free to study the collections. One of the purposes of this section is to provide a sampling of these documents for home study. Many of the embroideries in the following pages are shown in enlarged photographs so that the stitches are clearly visible.

These stitches and samples are not only shown for study purposes, but are intended to provide needleworkers with ideas for creative application to their own projects. It is not always enough to know how to do a particular stitch — it's sometimes helpful to see how someone else used it, suggesting the "where" and "how" for one's own work. There are literally hundreds of embroidery stitches; I've illustrated only some of those that appeared most frequently in the documents I studied in the Museum's collections. Many are familiar; some, I suspect, are not.

Just as there are different stitches, there are also different ways of working the same stitch. The instructions provided are the ones I find the easiest, after much trial and research. When trying a stitch for the first time, work it through carefully by doing the "in" and "out" motions of the needle in separate steps. Once the stitch construction is understood, the two motions can often be combined to establish speed and a rhythm of working.

The stitches are listed alphabetically.

Back Stitch

This simple, familiar sewing stitch is used in embroidery primarily for outlines or as a foundation for other stitches. It is also a popular quilting stitch.

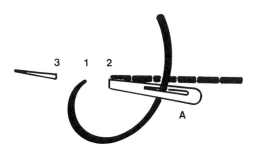

Diagram A. Working from right to left, begin the stitch by coming out on the outline at 1, a stitch length from the start of the line to be covered. Bring the needle in at 2 and out at 3. Go on to the next stitch by inserting the needle back into the first hole of the previous stitch and repeat steps 2 and 3. The beauty of the stitch is in the evenness and regularity of the stitches — it just takes a little practice.

The Brothers Bow Down before Joseph. *Enlarged detail from a Renaissance embroidery on natural-colored linen, worked in crimson silk threads. The figures in this scene from the biblical story of Joseph are worked in Back stitch, the background in Plait stitch. Italian, sixteenth century. Gift of Mrs. Harry G. Friedman, 1948.*

BARGELLO STITCH   See Florentine Stitch

BASKET WEAVE STITCH   See — under Tent Stitch — Diagonal Tent Stitch

Brick Stitch

This is a beautiful shading stitch that can be used on canvas and other fabrics. For even-weave fabrics, such as linen, use a blunt needle to make a slightly larger hole in the material; this is desirable because stitches in each row share the holes of the stitches in the preceding row. For canvas work in Brick stitch, as with most upright stitches, a heavier yarn is recommended to get good mesh coverage.

Enlarged detail from a crewel-embroidered bed hanging worked on cotton and linen twill in shades of blue, green, brown, and white. The rolling, shaded hills are worked in Brick stitch, the plants in Stem stitch. English, late seventeenth century. Rogers Fund, 1908. (The complete hanging is reproduced on page 56.)

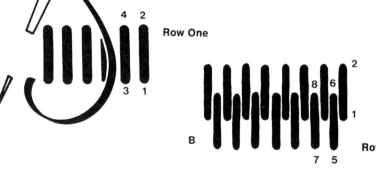

Diagram A. Brick stitch may be worked from left to right, right to left, or turned on its side and worked up and down. However, once a direction is established, it should be maintained for each row to keep stitches as straight as possible. Working from right to left, begin by making a row of vertical stitches coming out at 1 and going in at 2, out at 3 and in at 4, etc., leaving a space the thickness of one embroidery thread between each stitch. Continue until the desired row length is obtained.

Diagram B. Work the Second Row by coming out at 5 and going in at 6, a point halfway between the top and bottom of the stitches of the First Row, creating a stitch the same length as those in the First Row. Complete the row, again working from right to left.

Diagram C. For the Third Row, come out at 9 and go in at 10, in the lower hole created by the stitch in the First Row (thus 10 and 1 share the same hole). Complete the row in this fashion, working from right to left. Fill in the spaces in the first and last rows with half-length stitches.

145

Bukhara Stitch

This is a filling stitch which can be worked over large areas. Bukhara stitch is actually a form of couching, but instead of using two separate threads — one for filling and one for tying down the laid threads — the same thread is used continuously for both steps.

Floral detail from the border of a large cover, embroidered on natural-colored linen in red, green, yellow, and blue silk thread. The flowers are worked in Bukhara stitch; the leaves and outlines are in Chain stitch. Bukhara, Turkestan (Central Asia), seventeenth–eighteenth century. Gift of Miss Lily Place, 1921.

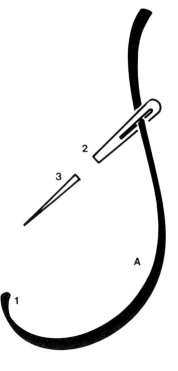

Diagram A. Begin by laying down the first thread, coming out at 1 and going in at 2. Be careful not to pucker the fabric by pulling the stitch too tight. Bring the needle out at 3, slightly to the left of and a short distance from 2.

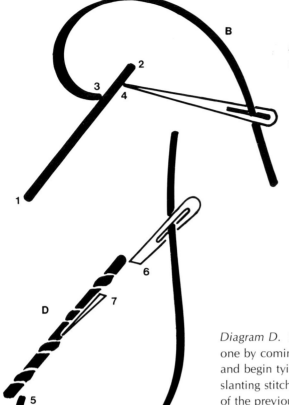

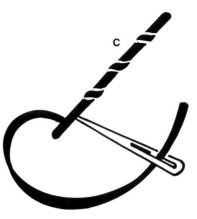

Diagram B. Complete the first tie-down stitch by making a small slanting stitch going in at 4.

Diagram C. Continue making small slanting stitches; space them equally along the length of the laid thread.

Diagram D. Lay the next thread close to the first one by coming out at 5 and in at 6. Come out at 7 and begin tying down the thread with small slanting stitches placed slightly below the stitches of the previous row.

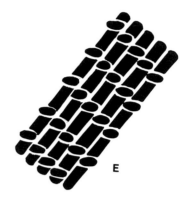

Diagram E. The finished effect of Bukhara stitch is a diagonally ribbed surface, created by the staggered rows of tie-down stitches.

Bullion Knot

This is a very tactile stitch which adds a varied texture to your embroidery when combined with flatter stitches. It is more suited to fairly coarse yarn than to cotton or silk thread. For best results, work with a fairly thick needle that has only a slight taper. It is easier to work Bullion Knot on a frame so that both hands are free to manipulate the needle and thread.

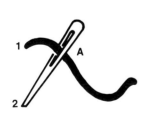

Diagram A. To begin, pierce the fabric from below coming out at 1. Bring the needle in at 2, creating the desired stitch length, but *do not pull the yarn through.*

Diagram B. Come out again into the same hole at 1, passing *only three-quarters* of the needle up through the fabric.

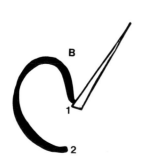

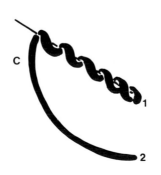

Diagram C. With your right hand hold the needle from below, and with your left hand begin to wind the loose loop of yarn in a counterclockwise direction around the needle. Wind it the number of times needed to fill the length of the stitch; the number of turns will depend on the thickness of the yarn and the length of the stitch.

Diagram D. Arrange the coils closely but *not tightly* by pushing them toward the eye of the needle. Hold them in place with your left thumb and index finger.

Diagram E. Still holding the coils, gently pull the needle up with your right hand, allowing the working yarn to pass through the coils.

Diagram F. Finish the stitch by going in with the needle at the end of the last coil, near 2.

Sunflower motif from a crewel-embroidered linen coverlet worked by Lucinda Coleman in tones of pink, brown, yellow, blue, and green. Lucinda, who is believed to have been Benjamin Franklin's niece, worked the center of the flower in tiny Bullion Knots. Other stitches used are Roumanian, Satin, and Stem. American, eighteenth century. Sansbury-Mills Fund, 1961.

Buttonhole Stitch

This familiar stitch is very versatile and has many decorative uses. It can be worked closely, widely spaced, in varying lengths and shapes — each method produces a different effect.

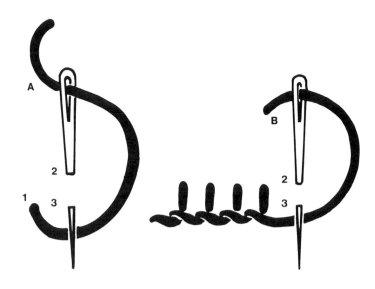

Diagram A. The stitch is worked from left to right. To begin, pierce the fabric from below and come out at 1. Hold the thread down with your left thumb and go in at 2, slightly to the right of and above 1. Bring the needle out at 3, directly below 2, passing the needle *over* the thread. Pull the thread downward to secure the loop.

Diagram B. Buttonhole worked with the stitches widely spaced — also known as Blanket stitch.

Diagram C. Buttonhole worked closely (Closed Buttonhole).

Diagram D. Buttonhole worked to fill a shape.

Enlarged detail from an embroidered linen cap worked in white linen thread. Done primarily in Closed Buttonhole and Buttonhole Wheel, which is Buttonhole stitch worked in a circular form, each stitch emanating from one central hole. The two border stitches are Square Chain and Feather stitch. Hungarian, eighteenth–nineteenth century. Rogers Fund, 1909.

Chain Stitch

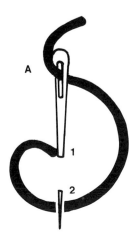

This stitch can be used as an outline stitch or as a filling stitch. If done as a filling stitch, work from the outline of the design toward the center of the shape to be covered; place each row parallel to the previous one. The stitches can be worked all in the same direction or (by turning the embroidery upside down after each row) in alternating up and down rows.

Diagram A. Begin by piercing the fabric from below coming out at 1. With the thread to the left of the needle, go back into the *same* hole at 1 forming a loop by holding the thread with your left thumb. Then come out at 2, passing the needle *over* the thread and pulling down to complete a chain loop.

149

Acrobat and Musician with Bagpipe and Drum. *Detail from an embroidered linen cover stitched in ecru-colored silk thread. Worked throughout in Chain stitch, it shows the ribbed effect created by doing Chain in alternating up and down rows. Spanish or Portuguese, sixteenth–seventeenth century. Gift of Mrs. William Bayard Cutting, 1945.*

Diagram B. For the next stitch insert the needle inside the previous loop at the exact point where the thread emerged from the first stitch, and repeat steps in Diagram A. Since the needle always goes back into the hole of the previous stitch, the reverse side of the embroidery will look like Back stitch.

Square or Open Chain Stitch

This is a lovely border stitch and a good one for filling stems and branches.

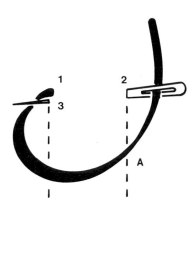

Diagram A. Bring the needle out on the left-side outline at 1. Hold the thread down with your left thumb and bring the needle in on the opposite outline at 2. Come out at 3, directly below 1, and pull the needle through, passing it *over* the thread.

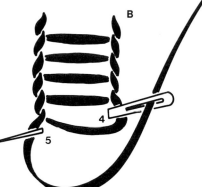

Diagram B. Holding the thread down with your left thumb and keeping the loop slightly slack, insert the needle inside the loop at 4, directly below 2. For the next stitch come out at 5, and repeat steps in Diagram A.

Carnation and Tulip. *Enlarged detail from an embroidered linen border worked in pink silk and silver thread. The stems are done in Square Chain; other stitches include Chain and Roumanian. Italian, eighteenth century. Anonymous Gift, 1879.*

Chinese Knot

Also known as Peking stitch, Chinese Knot has come to be called the "forbidden stitch" because it was traditionally worked so finely that many workers became blind. I don't know if these accounts are true, but apparently there is no basis to the claim that the stitch was "forbidden" by Chinese officials. There are, in fact, many more intricate and demanding stitches in Chinese embroidery.

When done with a needle of average size, Chinese Knot is a very textural stitch which can be worked loosely ("open"), to form looplike knots, or tightly ("closed"), forming a knot very similar to French Knot.

Goldfish and Underwater Plants. *Enlarged detail from an embroidered sleeveband worked on white satin in silk thread in tones of rose, yellow, brown, and green. The fish is stitched in hundreds of tiny Chinese Knots; the slightly open technique forms loops that suggest fish scales. The fish is outlined with a couched cord; the plants are worked in Satin stitch. Chinese, nineteenth century. Bequest of William Christian Paul, 1930.*

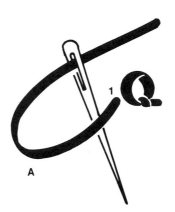

Diagram A. The stitch is worked from right to left. This diagram shows how to begin the stitch and indicates where the thread emerges from the previous stitch. For the first stitch, pierce the fabric from below coming out at 1. Hold the thread down with your left thumb and slip the needle between the thread and the fabric, forming a loop.

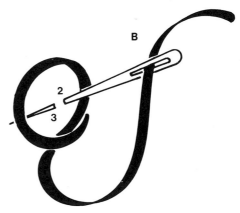

Diagram B. Insert the needle inside the loop piercing the fabric at 2, slightly to the left and above 1. Bring the needle out at 3 a short distance from 2, passing the needle *under* the thread. *Do not pull the needle through yet.*

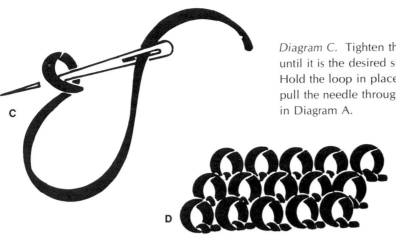

Diagram C. Tighten the loop around the needle until it is the desired size for the finished knot. Hold the loop in place with your left thumb and pull the needle through. Go on to the next stitch as in Diagram A.

Diagram D. Finished effect of Chinese Knots worked open as a filling stitch, with the knots placed close together and the rows staggered so that the stitches overlap slightly.

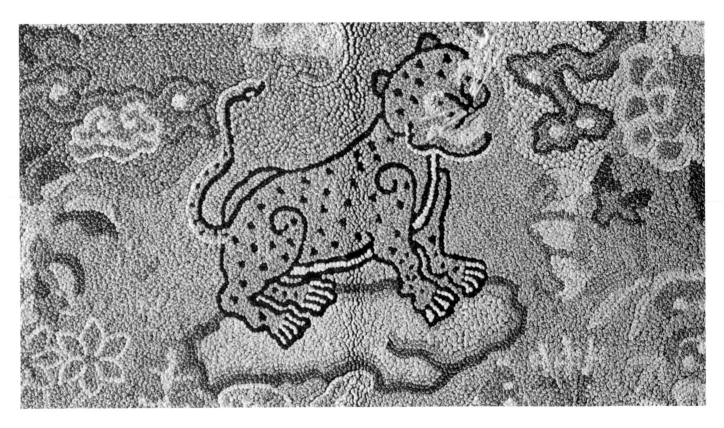

Leopard on a Rock. *Enlarged detail from a rank badge (insignia of a military official of the Third Rank) embroidered on silk cloth in colored silk thread. Worked throughout in Closed Chinese Knots. Chinese, late eighteenth–early nineteenth century. Bequest of William Christian Paul, 1930.*

CONTINENTAL STITCH   See Tent Stitch

Couching

Couching is a method of tying down laid threads with a separate contrasting thread. Since the laid threads merely "float" on the surface of the embroidery, it was a popular technique during the Middle Ages for the economical use of precious gold and silver threads in elaborate ecclesiastical embroidery. For the same reason it was also frequently used in the Orient for the embroidery on court robes and accessories. The stitch can be used for outlines or as a filling stitch. Decorative surfaces may be created not only by the arrangement of the laid threads, but also by the placement of the tie-down stitches.

Diagram A. Begin by laying one or more threads along the outline of the design. If several threads are used, smooth them so that they lie flat along the line. Thread the needle with a matching or contrasting texture or color, then come out at 1 and in at 2, making a tiny tie-down stitch. Continue working the length of the outline in this manner, spacing the small stitches evenly.

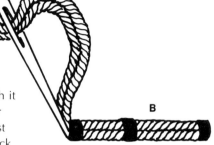

Diagram B. When the line of stitching is complete, finish it off by threading the loose ends in a large needle; anchor them by pulling them through the hole formed by the last couching stitch; run them under some stitches on the back before clipping off.

Enlarged detail of clouds from a Chinese rank badge embroidered on silk in gold thread and colored silk floss. The gold threads are couched with tiny silk tie-down stitches arranged in a brick pattern. Chinese, early Ch'ing dynasty, seventeenth century. Fletcher Fund, 1936.

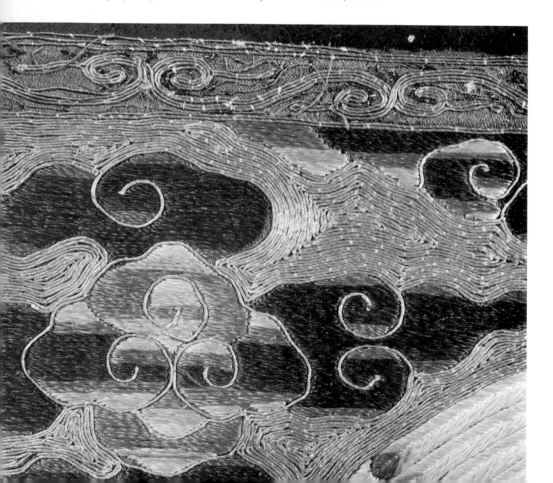

Cretan Stitch

I imagine this stitch derives its name from the beautiful Greek Island embroideries produced on Crete, where it was frequently used. It can be worked as a filling stitch by varying the width and angle of the stitches or as a wide border.

Flower and bird motif from the border decoration of a linen dress, embroidered in red silk thread with touches of green, yellow, and brown. The design is worked predominately in Cretan stitch with accents worked in Satin, Long-and-Short, Chain, and Stem. Greek Island (Crete), eighteenth century. Bequest of Richard B. Seager, 1926.

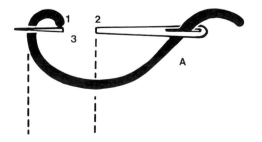

Diagram A. To work the stitch as a border decoration, pierce the fabric from below, coming out at 1 in the center of the border area. Holding the thread down to form a loop, go in at 2 on the right-hand outline. Bring the needle out at 3, slightly below and to the right of 1. Pull the thread through, passing the needle *over* the loop to complete the stitch.

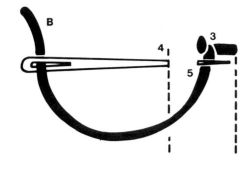

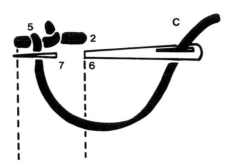

Diagram B. Form a loop and bring the needle in on the left-hand outline at 4 and out at 5, slightly below and to the left of 3. Again, complete the stitch by pulling the working thread through, passing the needle over the loop.

Diagram C. Repeat steps for Diagram A (6 should be almost touching 2) coming out at 7, slightly below and to the right of 5.

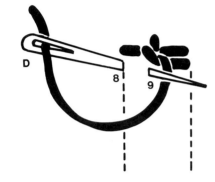

Diagram D. Continue working in this manner, alternating from side to side, to create a plaited effect down the center of the band.

Diagram E. Finished effect of Cretan stitch worked closed.

Diagram F. Finished effect of Cretan stitch worked open.

Cross Stitch

This well-known counted thread stitch brings to mind the charming seventeenth- and eighteenth-century European and American samplers that were part of every well-bred young lady's education. The stitch can be worked on even-weave fabric or canvas. For fabric, use a material with a well-defined mesh, so the stitches can easily be counted out. For a canvas stitch, use the double mesh (penelope). The stitch can be worked in either of the following two methods; use the one best suited to the section on your pattern.

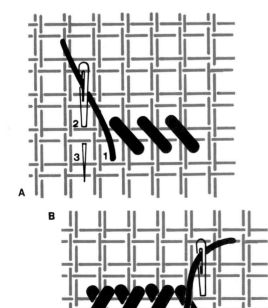

Diagram A. For the first and easier method of working Cross stitch, make a row of half cross stitches by coming out at 1 and going in at 2, then out at 3, directly below 2.

Diagram B. The stitches are completed by a return journey of half crosses slanting in the opposite direction; these share the holes of the stitches from the first journey. Be sure that the final half cross stitches always slant in the same direction — in this case, from lower left to upper right. When the stitch is worked in this method, the reverse side of the embroidery will look like upright stitches.

156

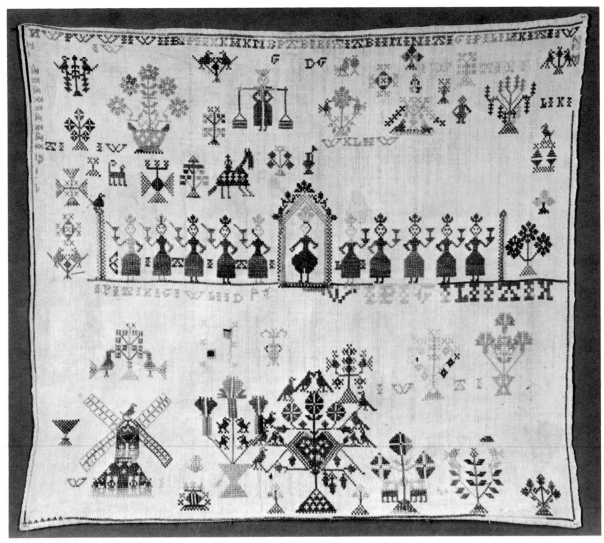

The Wise and Foolish Virgins with Bridegroom. *This motif is in the center of a delightful linen sampler embroidered in cream, green, blue, tan, and red silk. Worked throughout in Cross stitch. Dutch, eighteenth century. From the Collection of Mrs. Lathrop Colgate Harper, Bequest, 1957.*

Diagram C. The second method of working is by completing each cross before going to the next stitch. This is a more appropriate method for intricate patterns, and it is ultimately more practical, since the extra padding it provides on the reverse side of the embroidery will help prevent wear. It also produces a loftier appearance on the right side. Begin by coming out at 1, go over and in at 2 and out at 3, directly below 2. Complete the cross by going in at 4 and out at 5.

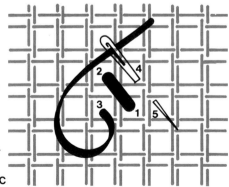

Diagram D. For the next stitch go back into the hole of the previous stitch at 6 and out at 7. Complete the cross as in Diagram C.

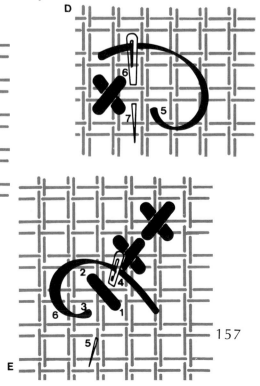

Diagram E. To work Cross stitch in a diagonal line, complete one stitch at a time by coming out at 1, in at 2, then out at 3 directly below 2. Cross the stitch by going in at 4 and out at 5 directly below 3. You are now in position for the next stitch.

157

Darning Stitch

This stitch can be worked as an easy filling for large background areas or in complicated geometric patterns — depending on patience and skill. It is basically a long running stitch that floats on the surface of the material with a small amount of fabric picked up between each stitch. Intricate patterns can be achieved by the progressive spacings of the "picked up" stitches. The stitch works best on material with a well-defined weave, so the threads can be easily counted out to secure even spacings and stitches.

Diagram A. This is a fairly simple darning stitch worked over five threads and under one thread. The stitches in the Second Row are staggered so that the picked-up threads fall in the center of the stitches in the First Row. The rows are worked alternately from top to bottom, bottom to top.

Diagram B. Working again over five threads and under one thread, a diagonal pattern is created by the steplike formation of the picked-up threads. This is achieved by picking up the thread directly below the one in the previous row.

Peacock from a linen valance embroidered in pale blue, red, yellow, and green silk thread. Worked throughout in Darning stitch, with the picked-up threads placed directly above the threads of the previous row, creating diagonal lines on the surface of the embroidery. Greek Island (Skyros), eighteenth century. Bequest of Richard B. Seager, 1926.

Diagram C. This method of working is known as Double Darning. It is particularly suited to a sheer fabric with a well-defined weave, since the finished embroidery is identical on both sides. Working from top to bottom, bring the needle out over five threads and under five threads, over five threads, etc., until the line is complete. Then, working from bottom up, fill in the spaces with a return journey going in and out of the holes of the stitches from the first journey. Be careful not to split the threads of the previous stitches.

Enlarged detail of processional figures from a horizontal panel. Embroidered on sheer cotton in silk thread in vivid shades of green, orange, blue, crimson, yellow, pink, green, and black, with accents in silver and silver-gilt thread. Worked predominately in Double Darning stitch, the picked threads of each row halfway between the stitches of the previous row. The embroidery is as perfect on the back as it is on the face. Indian, eighteenth century. Rogers Fund, 1959.

DIAGONAL TENT STITCH   See Tent Stitch

DOUBLE RUNNING STITCH   See Running Stitch

Feather Stitch

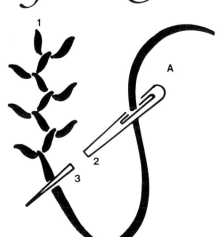

This is an easy stitch for stems, branches and leaf fillings. It is also a lovely border stitch.

Diagram A. Begin by piercing the fabric from below, coming out at 1. Go in at an angle at 2, holding the thread to make a loop; come out at 3, passing the needle *over* the thread. Make a corresponding stitch to the left of 1, again passing the needle over the thread. Continue working from side to side until the outline is complete. An example of Feather stitch used as a border decoration can be seen in the illustration for Buttonhole stitch.

Fishbone Stitch

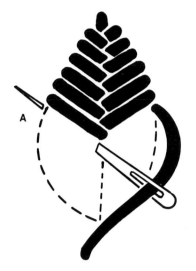

This can be worked as an attractive border when the stitches are equal in length, but it is more traditionally used as a leaf filling by graduating the lengths of the stitches to conform to the leaf outline.

Diagram A. To work a leaf shape, start with a small upright stitch by coming out at the tip; go in a short distance away on the center line. Bring the needle out on the right-hand outline close to the first stitch. Go in slightly to the left of the center line directly below the first stitch and out on the left-hand outline. To continue, bring the needle in just to the right of the center line below the previous stitch and out on the right-hand outline. Work from side to side until the shape is filled.

Florentine Stitch

For hundreds of years Florentine stitch has enjoyed enormous popularity among needleworkers. More commonly known as Bargello or Flame stitch, it is an easy canvas stitch that can be arranged in an unlimited number of vivid geometric designs. The basic stitch is Upright Gobelin worked in various patterns across the canvas. Use mono canvas unless a pattern specifies penelope.

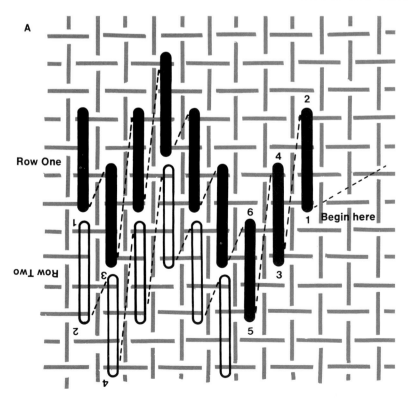

Diagram A. Florentine stitch is traditionally worked over four horizontal threads, but the length of the stitch may be varied. It is best to work all the rows in the same direction — in this case, from right to left. At the end of a row, either go back and begin the next row directly below the previous one (for a color change or if the thread has run out) or turn the canvas upside down and continue to work from right to left. Each row shares the holes of the stitches from the previous row.

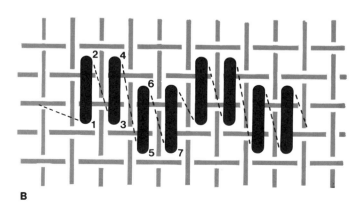

Intertwined ribbon design from a canvas embroidery in white, salmon, black, and yellow silk, worked in Florentine stitch. Probably Italian, eighteenth century. Gift of the United Piece Dye Works, 1936.

Queen Anne-style wing chair, covered on the front in needlepoint worked in blue, red, tan, and green wool. Embroidered throughout in Florentine stitch done in a trellis pattern. American, early eighteenth century. Gift of Mrs. J. Insley Blair, 1950.

Floral design from the border of an altar cover, embroidered on double-mesh canvas in blue, pink, brown, green, and white silk on a yellow ground. The background is worked in Florentine stitch, the flowers in Florentine, Satin, and Stem. Italian, seventeenth century. Gift of Susan Dwight Bliss, 1955. (For a pattern from the central portion of this piece, see page 116.)

Diagram B. This is the method of working Florentine stitch in horizontal rows. As shown here, it is done in groups of double stitches that cover two horizontal threads. Remember to turn the canvas for the next row so that stitches are always worked in the same direction — in this case from left to right. Again, each row shares the holes of the stitches from the previous row, as illustrated in Diagram A.

French Knot

Many a needleworker has been judged by the skill achieved in executing French Knots. Although they are not really difficult, they do require a bit of care and patience. Since they have a tendency to pull and unravel, it is essential that each knot be neat and tight. They can be worked packed closely together, as for fillings in flower centers and other areas, or used as dots of color and textural accents to break up an otherwise flat surface. An embroidery frame is helpful in working this stitch so that both hands are free to manipulate the thread and needle.

Enlarged detail of a flower from an embroidery on striped tan silk done in pastel-colored silk threads. The perfect tiny French Knots in the center of the flower beautifully contrast the flatter surfaces worked in variations of Satin stitch. French, nineteenth century. Rogers Fund, 1909.

Diagram A. Begin the knot by piercing the fabric from below, coming out at 1. With your right hand hold the needle in a horizontal position *above* the thread and with your left hand twist the thread once around the needle in an over/under motion.

Diagram B. With the point of the needle, go in at 2 almost in the same hole as 1 (but at least a fabric thread away). *Before* pulling the needle through to the wrong side, secure the loop snugly around it to hold the knot's shape. As the knot is held in place with your left thumb, gently pull the needle through to complete the stitch.

Diagram C. A completed French Knot. French Knots may be enlarged or reduced in size by varying the number of thread thicknesses used and the size of the needle, rather than by increasing the number of twists around the needle.

Gobelin Stitch

The ribbed appearance of this stitch closely resembles the surface of tapestry weaving. It derives its name from the renowned French manufactory of the Gobelins, a name that has become almost synonymous with the word "tapestry." It is a canvas stitch that can be used alone or in combination with other stitches to achieve a variety of textures. For example, it works well combined with Tent stitch in the same design. There are several ways of working Gobelin; two of these are illustrated and described below.

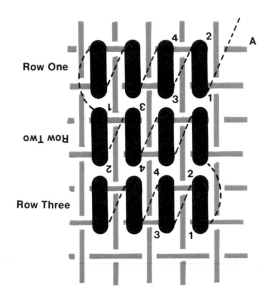

Diagram A (Upright Gobelin). This method is illustrated on mono canvas, each upright stitch covering two horizontal threads on the canvas. The stitch is shown worked from right to left, but it can be worked from left to right if more comfortable; however, once you have established the direction, do not alter it from row to row. To maintain the direction, turn the canvas upside down after each row, working the new row *into* the holes of the stitches from the previous row. Begin the stitch by coming out at 1. With a single motion of the needle, go in at 2 and out at 3, following the angle indicated by the sloping dotted line.

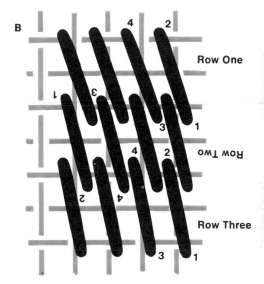

Diagram B (Encroaching Gobelin). Again, this stitch can be worked from right to left or from left to right, but the same direction must be maintained throughout; turn the canvas upside down after each row. The stitches are slightly diagonal, each row worked *between* the stitches of the previous row. To begin, come out at 1. Go in at 2, which is three horizontal threads above and one vertical thread to the left. Come out at 3, three horizontal threads directly below 2. For the Second Row, turn the canvas upside down and come out at 1, two horizontal threads above the stitches in the previous row. Count up three horizontal threads and over one vertical thread to the left; go in at 2 and out at 3 directly below 2. Follow the diagram for Row Three.

Unicorn with birds, flowers, fruit, and other animals. *Detail from a canvas-embroidered picture worked in colored wools with silk floss accents. The background is in Encroaching Gobelin stitch; the figures in Tent stitch. The areas in silk floss are couched in a trellis pattern. English, first half of the seventeenth century. Gift of Irwin Untermyer, 1964.*

163

Herringbone Stitch

This is one of the most ancient and versatile stitches. It can be used for thick outlines or as a filling stitch. Different effects can be achieved by working the stitches close together or by spacing them apart, allowing the foundation fabric to appear between the stitches.

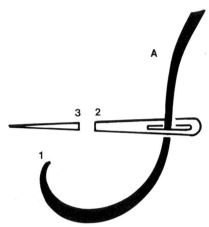

Diagram A. Herringbone stitch is worked from left to right. Begin by piercing the fabric from below coming out at 1. In one motion, bring the needle in on the opposite outline at 2 and out at 3, a short distance away.

Bird and flower motif from a linen embroidery worked in deep blue silk floss. This is an excellent example of Closed Herringbone stitch worked as a filling stitch. Greek Island (Crete), eighteenth century. Bequest of Richard B. Seager, 1926.

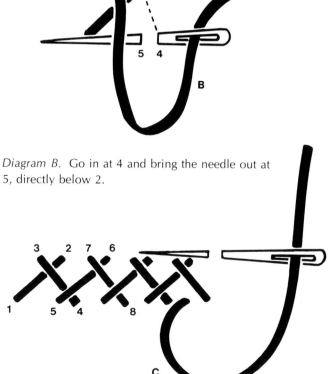

Diagram B. Go in at 4 and bring the needle out at 5, directly below 2.

Diagram C. Continue working in this manner until the shape is filled.

Diagram D. If the stitch has been done correctly, the reverse side will be parallel rows of evenly spaced horizontal stitches.

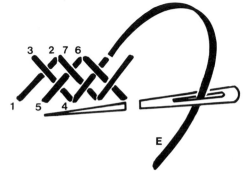

Diagram E. Closed Herringbone is worked exactly in the same manner, except that the crosses (2, 7) meet at the top and bottom. Since the needle is always coming out *into* the holes of the previous cross stitches, the reverse side of the work will look like parallel rows of Back stitch.

Diagram F. Finished effect of Closed Herringbone.

ℋungarian Point

This is a canvas stitch consisting of three upright stitches — a short, a long, and a short. If worked as a background filling, it produces a lovely texture of tiny diamonds across the surface of the embroidery. It may also be used for bold geometric designs and patterns.

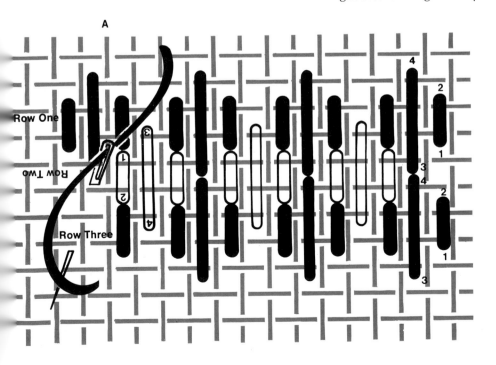

Diagram A. The stitch is normally done in horizontal rows. The diagram shows the rows worked in two colors simply to illustrate the stitch more clearly. Working from right to left, begin the First Row by coming out at 1 and going in at 2, making a short upright stitch over two horizontal canvas threads. Then make a long stitch over four horizontal threads; complete the first group with another short stitch over two horizontal threads. *Skip two vertical threads* and begin the next group of three stitches. Continue working in this manner until the row is complete. For the Second Row, to maintain the same working direction of right to left, turn the canvas upside down and bring the needle out into the first small stitch in the last group of stitches from the preceding row. Complete the stitch and finish the row from right to left, skipping two vertical threads between each stitch group. Turn the canvas right side up and begin the Third Row four horizontal threads below the first stitch in Row One as illustrated.

Laid Work

In laid work, long strands of thread are floated along the surface of the fabric; these are held in place with threads laid down in the opposite direction and secured with tiny tie-down stitches. Like couching, this was a popular and economical technique for working in precious gold and silk, since very little thread is wasted on the reverse side of the embroidery.

Man and Woman Playing Guitars. *Detail from a linen fiesta banner embroidered in silk floss in tones of pink, blue, yellow, and green. Most of the embroidery is laid work; other stitches include Stem and Herringbone. Spanish or Portuguese, eighteenth century. Gift of Mrs. Edward S. Harkness, 1941.*

Diagram A. Begin by laying down the threads in the manner indicated, coming out at 1 and in on the opposite outline at 2. Bring the needle out at 3, almost touching 2, and in on the opposite outline at 4. The threads should be kept fairly loose so that they lie flat and straight. At this stage the stitch looks like Satin stitch, but if you turn to the back of the work you will see that the long stitches are not carried across the reverse side as they are in Satin.

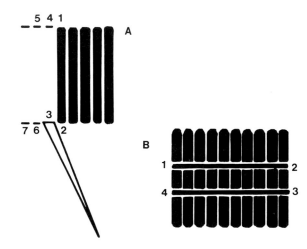

Diagram B. After the entire area is covered with long floating stitches, begin laying a series of threads in an opposing direction, widely spaced across the filled-in area. These can be placed horizontally, as shown here, or on the diagonal. To lay the horizontal threads come out at 1; carry the thread across the filled-in area and go in at 2. Bring the needle out at 3 and go in at 4 on the opposite side.

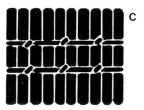

Diagram C. Now secure the horizontal laid threads with tiny slanting stitches, worked at even intervals.

Long-and-Short Stitch

This is a variation of Satin stitch used to achieve beautiful shaded effects.

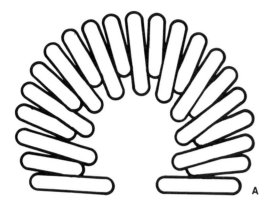

Diagram A. Beginning at the outline of the design, make a row of long and short stitches, radiating them to conform to the shape you are covering. The short stitch should be about three-quarters of the size of the larger one.

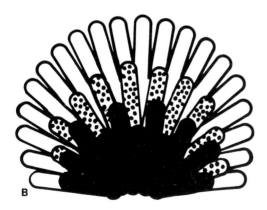

Diagram B. The shape is completed with long Satin stitches of *equal* length. Begin the Second Row with the next color tone, working the stitches a third of the way back into the short stitches in the previous row. With the dark shade, fill in the remaining spaces, working the long stitches back into the stitches in the previous row. As the shape narrows, you will need fewer stitches. If necessary, use smaller stitches for the final row to conform to the shape of the design.

Cupid. Detail from an embroidered cushion worked on white silk in silk threads in tones of red, pink, green, yellow, blue, and white. The central picture is worked in Long-and-Short stitch. English, seventeenth century. Rogers Fund, 1929.

167

Mosaic Stitch

This is an excellent canvas stitch for filling in background areas; it is quick to work and produces an overall texture of tiny squares on the surface of the embroidery. It is actually Hungarian Point worked on the diagonal, and like Hungarian, it consists of three stitches — two short and one long.

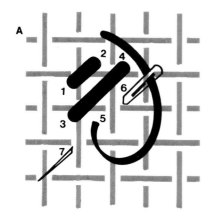

Diagram A. The stitch is shown here worked in vertical rows, always from top to bottom. The rows are worked from right to left. To begin, come out at 1 and go in at 2. Bring the needle out in the hole directly under 1 and make a long diagonal stitch by going in at 4, directly to the right of 2. Bring the needle out at 5, directly to the right of 3 and below 2. Complete the second small stitch by going in at 6, directly below 4. Come out at 7 directly below 3, and you are now in position to begin the next group of three stitches.

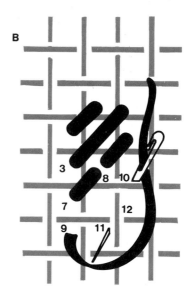

Diagram B. The first short stitch always begins directly below the long stitch from the previous group. Continue working as described in Diagram A until the row is complete.

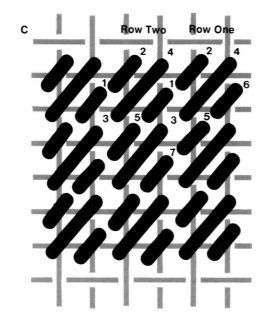

Diagram C. To work the next row, count two vertical threads to the left of the first stitch in Row One and come out at 1 in Row Two. Go in with the needle at 2 and out at 3 directly below 1. Complete the first group of three stitches; note that the small second stitch goes into the hole of the first stitch in Row One. Continue working in the manner described in Diagrams A and B, going back into the holes of the stitches in the previous row. If the stitch has been done correctly, each long stitch will share the hole with its counterpart in the previous row, and the second short stitch will share the hole with the first short stitch in the previous row.

Pekinese Stitch

If you are using Pekinese stitch for filling, always work from the outline of the design toward the center of the shape being covered.

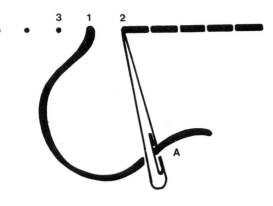

Diagram A. Begin by making a foundation row of Back stitches on the outline of the design.

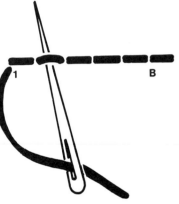

Diagram B. Using the same or a different color thread, come out at 1, just below the end of the last Back stitch. Pass the needle under the second stitch without piercing the fabric.

Diagram C. Bring the needle around and slip it under the first stitch, passing the needle *over* the thread.

Spotted Frog. *Enlarged detail from a sleeveband embroidered on pale blue satin in silk in tones of gray, white, green, red, and black, with accents in gold thread. Worked predominately in Pekinese stitch, dotted with tiny Chinese Knots. Chinese, nineteenth century. Bequest of William Christian Paul, 1930.*

Diagram D. Go back into the second stitch, again passing the needle over the thread.

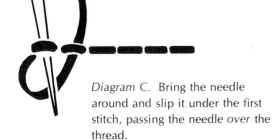

Diagram E. Continue lacing the thread around each stitch until the line is complete. Since the lacing is on the face of the work, the reverse side will only show a row of Back stitches.

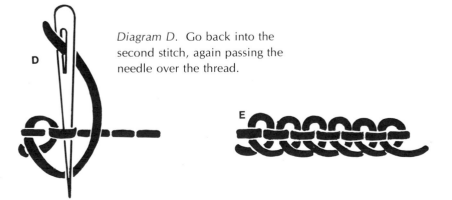

Peruvian Loop Stitch

On the surface, this ancient stitch looks very similar to Chain or Plait stitch; however, its execution is quite different. It is constructed like a continuous series of figure eights.

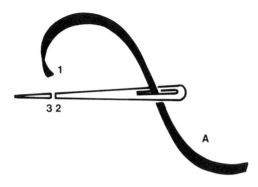

Diagram A. The stitch is worked in rows, from top to bottom. Begin by piercing the fabric from below, coming out at 1. With the thread above the needle, go in at 2 a short distance below, and come out at 3, making a small horizontal stitch the length of at least one fabric thread.

Diagram B. Make the first loop by passing the needle under the vertical stitch without piercing the fabric. Draw the needle through, but don't pull the loop too tight.

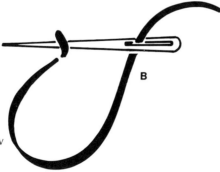

Diagram C. Make the next small horizontal stitch below by going in at 4 and out at 5. Pull the needle through, passing it *under* the thread.

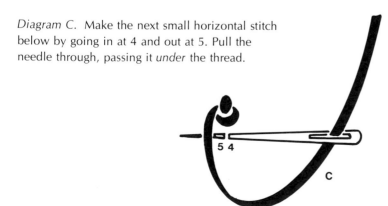

Indian with Feathered Headdress. *Enlarged detail of an embroidery worked on brown cotton in yellow, rose, mauve, and green wool. Worked throughout in Peruvian Loop stitch. Peruvian, Late Chimu Culture, 1100–1400. Gift of George D. Pratt, 1933. (For pattern from this design, see page 75.)*

170

Diagram D. Pass the needle under the looped stitch above without piercing the fabric.

Diagram E. Continue working in this manner by making a small horizontal stitch; then pass the needle under the previous loop without piercing the fabric as in Diagram D.

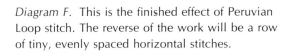

Diagram F. This is the finished effect of Peruvian Loop stitch. The reverse of the work will be a row of tiny, evenly spaced horizontal stitches.

Plait Stitch

This stitch can be worked on fabric with a well-defined weave or on canvas. It is an easy and quick stitch to use for filling background areas in canvas work, and a lovely border stitch on all fabrics.

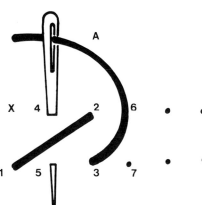

Diagram A. The stitch is worked from left to right. To begin, pierce the fabric from below and come out at 1. Make a diagonal stitch by going in at 2 and bringing the needle out at 3, directly below 2. Cross over the diagonal stitch and go in with the needle at 4, halfway between the mark "X" and 2, and come out at 5, directly below 4.

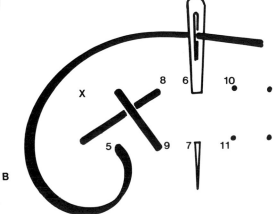

Diagram B. For the next stitch, go in at 6 and bring the needle out directly below at 7. Go in with the needle at 8 (the same hole as 2) and out at 9 (the same hole as 3).

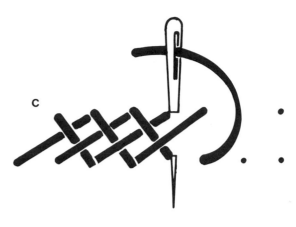

Diagram C. Continue working in this manner until the shape is filled.

Stylized flower motif from a linen embroidery worked in red silk thread. Worked throughout in Plait stitch. Greek Island, eighteenth century. Rogers Fund, 1909.

Diagram D. If the stitch has been worked correctly, the reverse side will show a row of parallel upright stitches.

Rococo Stitch

Found on many seventeenth- and eighteenth-century English embroideries, this elegant canvas stitch can be used today for simple geometric and floral patterns. The stitch works up beautifully in cotton thread, and the lighter shades tend to show it to better advantage. At first glance, the stitch looks very complicated, but work it through — it is actually very simple to do.

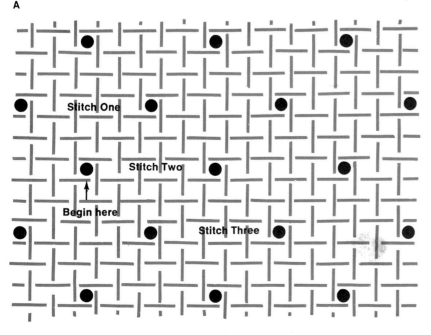

Diagram A. Working on mono canvas, take a pointed object — like a knitting needle or the end of a narrow watercolor brush — and enlarge the spaces on the canvas in the pattern indicated by black dots on the diagram. The enlarged spaces will form equal diamond shapes, six horizontal threads high and six vertical threads wide. These holes represent the top and bottom points of each stitch, and once they have been made, it will not be necessary to count out each stitch as you work. The openings are also an essential part of the character of the finished embroidery. You don't have to enlarge holes all over the canvas before you begin; this can be done in the course of the work. Just enlarge enough spaces to get the pattern started.

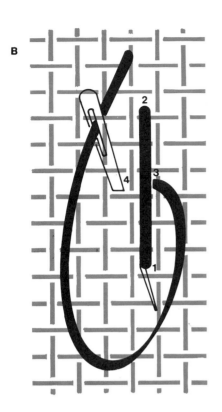

B

Diagram B. Begin the first stitch in the diamond at upper left (see Diagram A). The stitch consists of six long strands emanating from the same set of top and bottom holes, with three strands tied to the left and three strands tied to the right. To start, bring the needle out at 1 and go in at 2. With the thread to the left of the needle, come out at 3, three horizontal threads directly below 2. Make the first tie-down stitch to the left by going in at 4, one vertical thread to the left of 3, and bring the needle out again at 1.

Diagram C. With the thread to the left of the needle, go in at 2 and come back out at 4; pull the needle through, passing it *over* the thread. Go in at 5, one vertical thread to the left of 4, and back out at 1. This completes the second tie-down stitch to the left. Complete the third one by going back into 2, out again at 5, and in at 6. Bring the needle back out at 1; you are now in position to begin the three tie-down stitches to the right.

C

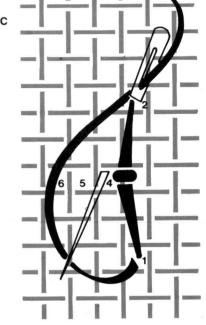

Enlargement of a vase from a canvas-embroidered cushion cover, worked in polychrome silk and silver thread. The sections of the vase worked in Rococo stitch are pierced with tiny openings. The other areas on the vase are worked in Tent stitch; the background is Encroaching Gobelin stitch. English, second quarter of the seventeenth century. Gift of Irwin Untermyer, 1964.

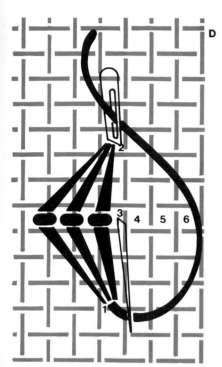

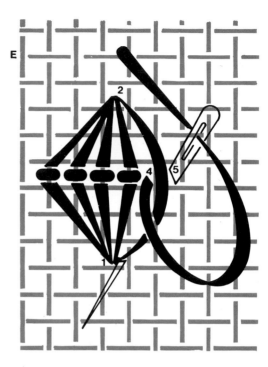

Diagram D. With the thread to the right of the needle go back into 2 and come out again at 3, three horizontal threads directly below 2. Pull the needle through, passing it over the thread. Complete the first tie-down stitch to the right by going in at 4 and coming out at 1.

Diagram E. Complete the second tie-down stitch to the right by going back into 2 and coming out again at 4, then in at 5. Bring the needle out at 1 and finish the third tie-down stitch to the right. Stitch One has been completed. Work the next stitch (see Diagram A) in the same way. Note that if the stitch is worked vertical to the canvas, like the stitch just worked, the right side hole of the first stitch becomes the top hole of the second stitch (see Diagram F). Work the stitches in diagonal rows so that the thread does not block the openings and spoil the finished effect of the embroidery. If the rows are worked from upper left to lower right, do the tie-down stitches to the left first as described in Diagrams B through E; however, if the rows are worked from upper right to lower left, then begin with the tie-down stitches to the right, so that the thread doesn't have to travel far for the next stitch.

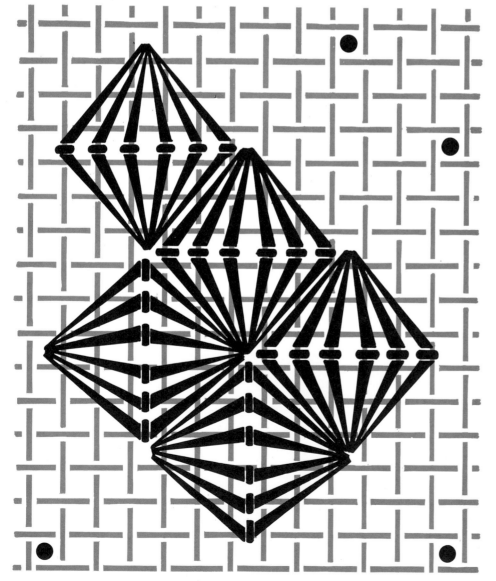

Diagram F. This is the finished effect of Rococo stitch. The stitch can be worked vertical to the canvas, or by turning the canvas forty-five degrees, horizontal. The combination of the two directions produces a beautiful effect.

F

Roumanian Stitch

Many beautiful examples of Roumanian stitch can be found on the crewel-embroidered bed hangings and chair coverings that decorated the homes of our colonial ancestors. The stitch was favored for economy's sake, since unlike Satin stitch, very little thread is wasted on the back of the embroidery. This stitch is often referred to as "Oriental stitch," probably because it was used in designs inspired by Oriental motifs.

Basket of Flowers. *A motif from a crewel-embroidered linen bedspread worked by Mary Breed of Breed's Hill, Boston, in tones of pink, yellow, blue, and green. The flowers and leaves are worked in Roumanian stitch, the stems in Herringbone, and the basket in Stem stitch done in a lattice pattern. American, dated 1770. Rogers Fund, 1922.*

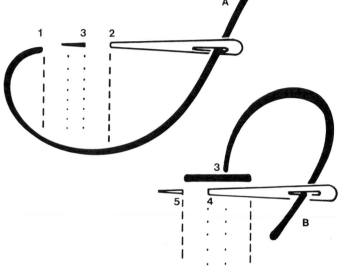

Diagram A. To begin, come out on the left outline of the shape at 1. With the thread *below* the needle go in on the right outline at 2 and come out at 3.

Diagram B. Make a small slanting stitch by going in at 4; bring the needle out on the left outline at 5 — almost touching 1 — so that there are no spaces between the stitches.

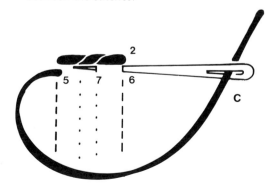

Diagram D. This is the finished effect of Roumanian stitch. The reverse side of the work will be two rows of tightly packed horizontal stitches.

Diagram C. With the thread below the needle, go in on the right outline at 6, almost touching 2, and come out at 7, directly below 3. Complete the stitch as shown in Diagram B. Continue working in this manner until the shape is filled.

Running Stitch

This simple stitch is familiar to all home sewers. It is the easiest of the outline stitches and is the basic stitch used for smocking.

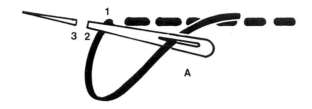

Diagram A. Working from right to left, come out with the needle at 1 and go in at 2, a stitch-length away. Bring the needle out at 3 and continue working in this way until the outline is complete. The stitches should all be the same size and evenly spaced.

Double Running Stitch

This stitch is also known as Holbein stitch because it appears on many of the embroidered costumes found in the portraits by the famous German court painter. It is an easy outline stitch that is suitable for transparent fabrics because its appearance is identical on both front and back.

Enlargement of dancing figures on an embroidered linen border worked in crimson silk thread. The design is worked predominately in Double Running stitch; the background is a drawn fabric stitch. Italian, seventeenth century. Gift of Harry C. Friedman, 1947.

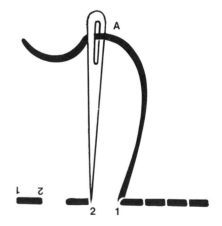

Diagram A. Working from right to left, make a series of Running stitches evenly spaced one stitch length apart. Turn the work upside down and fill in the spaces with a second journey of Running stitches, going back into the holes of the stitches from the first journey.

Satin Stitch

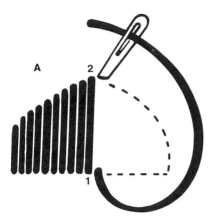

Basic Satin stitch dates back to ancient times, but many variations of the stitch have developed over the centuries. Although the construction of the stitch is very easy, the beginner may find it difficult to create even stitches — this comes with practice. The smooth appearance of Satin stitch may be enhanced by combining it with a variety of contrasting textures.

Diagram A. To cover a shape in Satin stitch, begin on the bottom outline coming out at 1. Go in on the top outline at 2, come out again on the bottom outline. The stitches should be barely touching — not overlapping. Gradually lengthen and shorten each stitch to conform to the shape of the design.

Diagram B. Satin stitch can also be worked on the diagonal. In this case it is easier to maintain the slant by coming out at 1 on the top outline and in at 2, back out at 3, etc.

Detail of an embroidered mirror case worked on fine gauze in red, green, white, and black silk thread. Worked in Satin stitch on counted mesh. Chinese, nineteenth century. Bequest of William Christian Paul, 1930.

Spray of flowers from a tailor's sample for an embroidered waistcoat worked on deep green velvet in white and brown silk floss, with accents of brown chenille, gold thread, gold purl, and paillettes. Worked in Satin stitch contrasted with a variety of textures. French, early nineteenth century. Gift of the United Piece Dye Works, 1936.

Seed Stitch

This is an airy filling stitch that works well in combination with other stitches to create a variety of textures.

Diagram A. Work small, even straight stitches in any direction until the area is covered. The stitches should be randomly placed to achieve an overall tonal effect.

178

Enlargement of fantastic flowers on an embroidered linen skirt worked in silk thread in shades of blue, rust, and gold. The middle tones of the flowers are done in Seed stitch; other stitches include Long-and-Short, Satin, Stem, laid work, and laced filling stitches. English, early eighteenth century. Everfast Fund, 1973.

Split Stitch

Split stitch looks like an elongated Chain stitch, although it is not a loop formation. The thread is actually split in half for each stitch. It is ideal for thin outlines and delicate details. It can also be used as a filling stitch when worked in parallel rows, and by varying the colors in each, gradual shaded effects can be achieved. Beautiful examples of this method of shading can be found on medieval church embroideries.

Madonna and Child. *Detail of a panel from a chasuble, worked on unbleached linen in colored silk and silver-gilt thread. The Madonna's robe is stitched in shaded rows of Split stitch. In this particularly interesting detail you can also see the preliminary underpainting and the way linen floss padding is couched down before it is covered over with silks or metallic thread — a technique used to create a raised or sculptured effect. Italian, second half of the 14th century. Gift of Irwin Untermyer, 1964.*

179

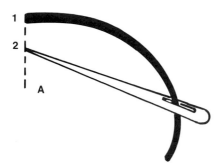

Diagram A. The stitch is worked from top to bottom or from left to right. To begin, pierce the fabric from below coming out at 1. Go in on the outline at 2 — the distance of the desired stitch length.

Diagram B. To complete the stitch, bring the needle out again into the center of the straight stitch, splitting the thread up the middle. Pull the needle through and go on to the next stitch. Keep all the stitches the same size. If you are using Split stitch for filling, begin on the outline of the design and work toward the center of the shape being covered.

Stem Stitch

Stem stitch — as the name indicates — is a line stitch. However, it can also be worked in parallel rows as a filling stitch.

Pumas. Enlarged detail from an embroidered border worked on woolen cloth in green, blue, and tan wool. The entire design is worked in Stem stitch used as a filling stitch. From Paracas, possibly Peruvian (Early Nazca Culture), second–sixth century A.D. *Gift of George D. Pratt, 1933.*

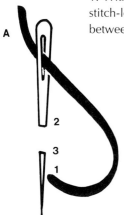

Diagram A. To begin, bring the needle out on the outline at 1. With the thread to the right of the needle go in at 2, a stitch-length away. Bring the needle out at 3, halfway between 1 and 2.

180

Diagram B. Go in on the outline at 4, at a point away from 3 equal in length to the length of the first stitch, and come out into the same hole at 2. Continue working in this manner until the outline is complete. As the stitch is worked, remember to keep the thread to the right of the needle, and always come out into the hole of the previous stitch.

Tent Stitch

This is the most commonly used canvas stitch. It is more easily worked on mono canvas than on penelope and consists of slanting stitches, each of which covers one mesh on the canvas.

Petit point (Tent stitch) embroidery, possibly designed for one side of an elbow pillow. Worked on loosely woven gauze in shades of blue, white, pink, green, and purple silk, with accents in gold-wrapped thread. Chinese, nineteenth century. Gift of Mrs. Nellie B. Hussey, 1942.

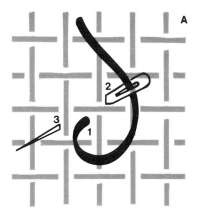

Diagram A. The stitch is *always* worked from right to left. Begin Row One by coming out at 1. Make a diagonal stitch by going in at 2, covering one mesh, and bring the needle out at 3, one vertical thread to the left of 1. Continue working in this manner to complete the First Row.

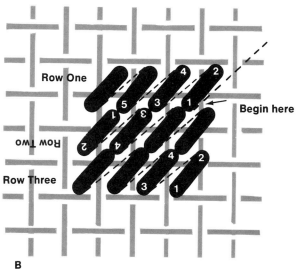

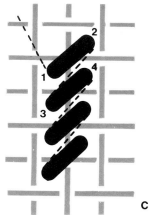

Diagram B. For Row Two, turn the canvas upside down and continue working from right to left. The stitches in the Second Row share the holes of the stitches of the First. For Row Three, turn the canvas right side up and continue working from right to left, going back into the holes of the stitches of the previous row.

Diagram C. Tent stitch worked as a vertical outline.

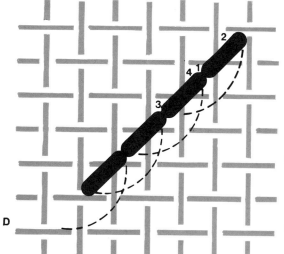

Diagram D. Tent stitch worked as a diagonal outline slanting from upper right to lower left produces a straight, unbroken line.

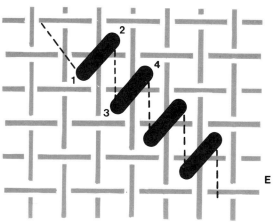

Diagram E. Tent stitch worked as a diagonal outline slanting from upper left to lower right produces a steplike broken line.

Diagonal Tent Stitch

This stitch is also known as Basket Weave because it is worked in a method that produces a woven basket effect on the reverse side. However, it looks exactly like basic Tent stitch on the face of the embroidery. It may be a difficult stitch to understand at first, but is worth mastering, since it has several advantages over Tent stitch. One of these is that the ''woven'' threads on the wrong side provide a more even padding for the embroidery, which enhances its appearance and helps prevent wear. Another advantage is that the canvas is not turned during the course of the work, which saves time. Finally, Diagonal Tent doesn't warp the canvas as much as Tent, and thus requires little or no blocking. However, Diagonal Tent stitch can only be used to fill in large solid areas. When working from a pattern, outline the shapes in Tent stitch, then fill in the larger areas in Diagonal Tent.

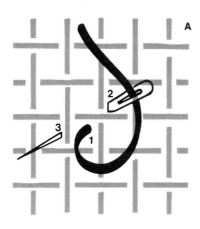

Diagram A. Diagonal Tent is worked in alternating *down* and *up* diagonal rows. Begin Stitch One as for basic Tent stitch by coming out at 1 and going in at 2; come out at 3 to the left of 1.

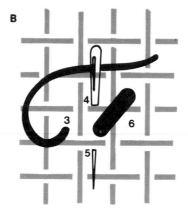

Diagram B. Bring the needle in at 4 and come out at 5, two horizontal threads directly below. Complete Stitch Three by going in at 6 and out at 7. This completes the first *down* row.

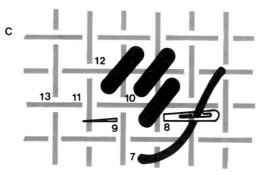

Diagram C. To begin the *up* row, complete Stitch Four by going in at 8, and with the needle in a horizontal position, come out at 9 (passing the needle behind Stitch Three). Complete Stitches Five and Six in the same manner (note that Stitch Five shares a hole with Stitch Two and Stitch Six shares a hole with Stitch One).

Diagram D. Begin the *down* row with Stitch Seven, directly to the left of Stitch Six. When working a *down* row, the needle is vertical to the top of the canvas. Come out at Stitch Eight, two horizontal threads directly below completed Stitch Seven (passing needle behind Stitch Six). Complete Stitch Eight by going into the bottom hole of Stitch Two. Complete Stitches Nine and Ten in the same manner. To begin the *up* row, do Stitch Eleven directly below Stitch Ten, and with the needle now in a horizontal position go on to Stitch Twelve (passing the needle behind Stitch Ten). To complete the *up* row do Stitches Thirteen, Fourteen and Fifteen; do Stitch Sixteen directly to the left of Fifteen to begin the *down* row. Continue working *down* and *up* rows until the shape is filled. If you lay your needlework aside for a while, it will be easier to see the direction to continue working in if you stop in the *middle* of a row.

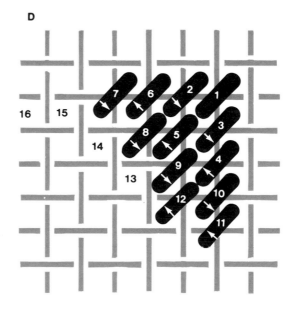

183

Selections for Further Reading and Reference

Anton, Ferdinand, and Dockstader, Frederick J. *Pre-Columbian Art*. New York: Harry N. Abrams, 1968.

Ashton, Leigh. *Samplers*. London and Boston: The Medici Society, 1926.

Cammann, Schuyler. "Embroidery Techniques in Old China." *Archives of the Chinese Art Society of America*, XVI (1962).

Davis, Mildred J. *Early American Embroidery Designs*. New York: Crown, 1969.

Fernald, Helen E. *Chinese Court Costumes*. Toronto: University of Toronto Press, 1946.

Gentles, Margaret. *Turkish and Greek Island Embroideries*. Chicago: The Art Institute of Chicago, 1964.

Groves, Sylvia. *The History of Needlework Tools and Accessories*. London: Country Life Limited, 1966.

Hackenbroch, Yvonne. *English and Other Needlework: Tapestries and Textiles in the Irwin Untermyer Collection*. Cambridge: Harvard University Press, 1960.

Harbeson, Georgiana Brown. *American Needlework*. New York: Coward-McCann, 1938.

Harcourt, Raoul d'. *Textiles of Ancient Peru and Their Techniques*. Seattle: University of Washington Press, 1962.

Hudson, G. F. *Europe and China*. London: Edward Arnold & Company, 1931.

Huish, Marcus B. *Samplers and Tapestry Embroideries*. London: Longmans, Green and Company, 1900.

Irwin, John, and Hall, Margaret. *Indian Embroideries*. India: S. R. Bastikar, 1973.

Johnstone, Pauline. *A Guide to Greek Island Embroidery*. London: Victoria & Albert Museum, 1972.

Kendrick, A. F. *English Needlework*. London: A & C Block Ltd., 1933.

Late Egyptian and Coptic Art. Text by J. D. Coney. Brooklyn: The Brooklyn Museum, 1943.

Little, Frances. *Early American Textiles*. New York and London: The Century Co., 1931.

Lewis, Suzanne. *Early Coptic Textiles*. Stanford: Stanford University, 1969.

Li, H. L. *The Garden Flowers of China*. New York: The Ronald Press Company, 1959.

Mead, Charles W. *Old Civilizations of Inca Land*. New York: American Museum of Natural History, 1924.

Means, Philip Ainsworth. *Peruvian Textiles*. New York: The Metropolitan Museum of Art, 1934.

Remington, Preston. *English Domestic Needlework*. New York: The Metropolitan Museum of Art, 1945.

Symonds, Mary, and Preece, Louisa. *Needlework Through the Ages*. London: Hodder and Stoughton, 1928.

Thompson, Dorothy. *Coptic Textiles*. Brooklyn: The Brooklyn Museum, 1971.

Vaclavik, Antonin, and Orel, Jaroslav. *Textile Folk Art*. London: Spring Books, n.d.

Wace, A. J. B. *Mediterranean and Near Eastern Embroideries*. 2 vols. London: Halton & Company Ltd., 1935.

Williams, C. A. S. *Outlines of Chinese Symbolism*. Peiping: Customs College Press, 1931.